REAL ESTATE

INVESTING AS A LUCRATIVE

HOBBY AND TAX SHELTER

YOUR GUIDE TO SUCCESS IN GENERATING CONSISTENT RENTAL INCOME

DARYL DELIMAN

ACTIVE REAL ESTATE INVESTOR SINCE 1984

authorHOUSE®

AuthorHouse™
1663 Liberty Drive
Bloomington, IN 47403
www.authorhouse.com
Phone: 833-262-8899

Published by AuthorHouse 10/11/2022

ISBN: 978-1-6655-7105-0 (sc)
ISBN: 978-1-6655-7104-3 (hc)
ISBN: 978-1-6655-7106-7 (e)

Library of Congress Control Number: 2022917164

Print information available on the last page.

CONTENTS

FOREWORD BY BOB KIENAST

In the multitude of books written on real estate investing, you will find that most provide a lot of information on a certain sector of real estate investing. Certainly valuable insight, but only Daryl's presentation addresses ALL of the many aspects of real estate investing.

He makes a real effort to "touch all the bases " with real examples. Real estate investing is multifaceted. Perhaps you select the right property at the right time, but poor financing has you in negative cash flow. Maybe you're off to a good start with the right property and good financing, but select the wrong tenant, leaving you without rental income for months, which can happen as today's courts are often pro tenant and postpone eviction. Maybe you're an excellent landlord, but economic conditions leave you with an unemployed tenant, hence no rental income.

No one person has expertise in all the aspects of real estate investing. Daryl relies on interviews with three very experienced experts in their respective fields. Their contributions are unique and enlightening,

Real Estate Investing as a Lucrative Hobby and Tax Shelter is a must read for the committed real estate investor as it presents all the required tools to build a real estate portfolio to ultimately secure financial freedom.

Will the inevitable downturn sink your real estate investing plans, or can you minimize damage and weather the storm? Plan for long-term real estate investing to create financial wealth and stability for the rest of your life.

INTRODUCTION

While growing up in eastern "flatland" Torrance, my older brother and I dreamt of, spoke of, planned for someday getting wealthy enough to move up, literally and figuratively, to the hills of Palos Verdes or bordering Rolling Hills Estates. As two of five children of an LA city school teacher, no major improvement was forthcoming or financially possible. We would ride our bicycles through Palos Verdes, enjoy the ocean views and fantasize about the house we would own someday in this idyllic Southern California residential setting.

Later in high school, this financial or class structure was reinforced when I was dating a girl from Rolling Hills high school. She justified dating me, a" flatlander", to her friends and family as my status was improved because I had been accepted to Annapolis. Curious to listen to her present me, but not unexpected.

While working as a Western regional manager for major companies in the field of scientific lab equipment, I became a multimillionaire by investing in Southern California real estate. I benefited by utilizing tax advantages for sheltering income, hence allowing for more seed money to acquire additional properties. In this book, I offer pragmatic steps for selecting ideal properties, financing, screening prospective tenants, upgrading properties by including accessory dwelling units (ADUs), and expanding a real estate portfolio while maintaining positive cash flow.

If you're looking to get rich quick by house-flipping or other high-risk strategies—wrong book. This plan, or plans, is low-risk but requires patience and persistence. Seed money and/or excess income, good credit, and endorsing support staff are required.

Perhaps you can benefit from my thirty-plus years of real estate investing in Southern California, which includes acquiring many varied properties, upgrades of every sort, two recessions, one depression, an IRS audit, a BK Chapter 11 reorganization, various partners, evictions, and most possible real estate issues. Prudent responses are offered so the inevitable real estate downturn doesn't sink your plan.

Many working professionals, especially those of us in heavy-tax-burden states like California, are alarmed at the increasing tax bite on our hard-earned income and seek some legal relief. Also, everyone needs to plan for retirement, and rental income from investment properties will continue to increase; it's often your safest hedge against inflation. Both important goals can be achieved here.

Ready to get started in real estate investing? There are many benefits, and it often does not require major capital. My presentation includes specific successful plans and interviews with experts in the important areas of finance, property management, and tax shelters.

CHAPTER 1

Getting Started: Selecting the Property

Let's get started by selecting an ideal property with growth potential. There are more comments and insights on this very important topic throughout, and a basic assumption is that you are investing during a time of at least somewhat positive economic trends.

I usually favor houses, as there is less turnover, hence less attention required. Multiunit buildings may offer better cash flow while requiring more attention. Both offer a tax shelter advantage.

Ideally, your investment property should be within a one-hour drive of your residence. That's not always practical, but it will certainly be a benefit, not only in reducing your travel time and expenses but for another important reason. Who might take advantage of a remote property owner? Try everyone.

In chapter 3, Marty Prince tells us of an investment property he owned in another state where he thought the property manager was checking. He wasn't. Usually the case.

Next, the craftsmen you have working on your property will pad their bills when they realize you're too far away to inspect the work. Sure, you can ask for pictures, but they don't tell the whole story.

And, of course, tenants will abuse the property in every way possible, including not maintaining the yard, parking on the lawn, and packing the house with another family or two, as they recognize you are too remote to inspect.

Many years ago, an article in the *San Bernardino Sun* newspaper stated that even the county tax assessor would have higher assessments for properties with remote owners. I have twice challenged property assessments, with limited success, but at least the county tax assessor knew I was reviewing.

To further promote the concept of being a local property owner, you should have a phone number in the area code of your investment properties. I was pleasantly surprised that my cell phone carrier could add a second phone number to my existing iPhone at a fairly reasonable cost. I call tenants and others from this local area code.

How I Got Started

Our venture in building a family real estate portfolio began in the mid-'80s. My dad, Daniel, was a retired Los Angeles schoolteacher with some experience in owning rental properties—including one house, a triplex, and a duplex—over the previous ten years. My older brother Dennis was a real estate professional with broker's license as well as a jurist doctorate. He also had experience as a loan agent. I brought good credit and the strongest financial standing, thanks to my career selling lab equipment. Thus began Delinco Properties, as in *Del*iman *in*vestment *co*mpany.

Prudent real estate investing can benefit you in four ways, stated here in descending order of probable significance:

1. Appreciation—Study the demographics and economics of the area. If the property is selected prudently, it should increase in value. Upgrades always help with greater value increase.
2. Tax relief—Depreciation and other passive real estate losses can reduce your annual income tax payment, something especially needed by us Californians.
3. Positive cash flow—Use principle, interest, taxes, insurance, maintenance, and management (PITIMM) to assess and increase your rents annually, and/or with turnover. Positive cash flow should increase annually.

4. Amortization—If you've seen the graphs, the amortization of mortgages on investment property increases geometrically over time, depending on the interest rate and period of the loan.

Ideally, for all four items, we are assuming a married couple, both working and owning multiple properties; however, all advantages also apply to singles.

When we were just starting Delinco, we had interest in investing in Orange County as well as the IE (the Inland Empire, made up of San Bernardino and Riverside counties). We did have one house for a while in a less affluent area of Orange County (the OC). We started making comparisons and found the ratio of rent/PITIMM favored the IE. Specifically, we could easily get a 2′ ratio in the IE, where as in the OC, it was about 1.6. Also, any vacancy would be especially financially painful in the OC if it were vacant for a couple of months. Too risky for us, as we were just starting the business. We had to maintain credit to continue buying property, so timely mortgage payments were a must.

Appreciation of the value of your real estate investment depends on selecting an investment property in an area, and at a time, of increasing real estate values. For this parameter, you need to study the demographics, economics, and other information on the area. There's certainly no guarantee; for example, if you had purchased an investment home or most any real estate in 2007 at the peak of the market, you would have lost money when the market crashed (see chapter 14 on trends). There was no property purchase that would not have lost money in this universal real estate crash.

Graph 1. UC RIVERSIDE TODAY: INLAND EMPIRE CYCLES

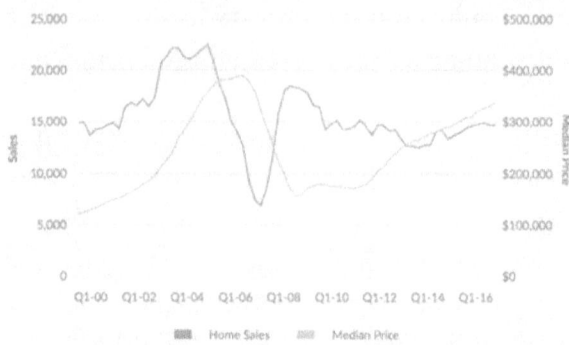

Source: https://inlandempire.us/
ucr-report-on-inland-empires-housing-market-cycle/

The Inland Empire's median home cost ballooned 78 percent to nearly $400,000 during the three years ending in 2019. Pricing remains a bargain compared to typical home prices of about $550,000 to $700,000 in the rest of Southern California.

Update late 2022 Inland Empire had a year-over-year price gain of 17.9 percent, with the median price being $539,000. California is still a seller's market, and home prices have reached record highs across all the regions due to tight supply. Nearly two-thirds of homes sold above the asking price in November.

Overall, the IE is more of a blue collar area adjacent to affluent Orange County and financially diverse Los Angeles County, so the IE always has considerably lower real estate costs. Typically, the IE median home price is 60 percent of Orange County's and 72 percent of Los Angeles County's home prices. Hence, the IE seemed to be our best area in which to invest.

In contrast, note how rapidly prices increased after the tremendous real estate crash of 2007. If you were fortunate enough to be liquid at this time and buying houses, you would certainly have benefited from the rapid appreciation of real estate values. These quickly increasing times after this tremendous real estate crash spawned a series of irritating television programs. You may remember flipping houses or buying foreclosures or something involving greed. Of course, in that time of quickly inclining real estate values, everyone was making money. Some are still flipping houses profitably, according to their current TV show.

I say *irritating*, as it seemed that everyone had an interest in the quick buck and no long-term interest in holding or improving properties. Also irritating, and I think misleading, was the fact that these were anomalous real estate times. Look at the graph. This sort of rapid incline in price cannot be sustained long-term. This fact was rarely noted, thus leaving the impression that this was typical of real estate investing.

As the cycles of real estate would suggest, our procedures of obtaining property have changed greatly over the years. When Delinco started, in the mid-1980s, interest rates were in the low teens, which seem to trigger a recession. Put these two factors together (high interest rates and recession), and people were simply walking away from their houses and their loans.

Foreclosures causing boarded-up houses were common. HUD and other federal agencies reclaimed these houses through foreclosure. HUD would then group together about fifteen houses and offer to sell to investors with a hefty down payment but good loan terms for five years. Delinco did not have that type of capital back then, so we bought a block of twelve houses secondhand from a wealthier investor who was tired of landlording. I had to secure this purchase by offering collateral with my residence, as we had very little capital.

Dennis and I were a convincing team, promising to immediately upgrade the houses and enroll good tenants. It was an excellent start to Delinco, and after some bumps in the road, we did secure financing and managed to keep ten of the twelve houses. Most are still excellent rentals for us. Of course, my residence was released by the wealthier investor after financing was secured.

Geographic Selection Considerations

There are many aspects to the project of selecting property. First, let's look at general geography. Is this an area that is enjoying economic growth and expansion in real estate? Some states are actually having a decrease in population. There could be some important economic factors to consider, such as unemployment rate. It's always a good plan to see what business expansion might be planned for the area that might significantly add to employment.

Also, check our country's current macroeconomic outlook. More on this topic in chapter 14 on trends. While we certainly are in totally different economic times today, I keep coming back to cycles in real estate.

Next, how would you classify the particular area in which you want to invest? Let's try three categories: almost slum, blue-collar, and upscale. Each has its advantages and disadvantages:

- Almost slum
  - Disadvantages
    - Tenants may be financially irresponsibleand usually late with rent.
    - Landlord or property manager may need to collect the rent in person.
    - Tenants may be difficult to work with and can be dangerous.
    - Tenants will probably damage property more than expected.
    - Screening tenants is a major chore. Section 8 (see chapter 8) may be the best alternative.
  - Advantages
    - You can obtain a real bargain in this area, but it's only an apparent bargain if you can't collect all the rents.
    - You can find a building or a house at a low price compared to the anticipated rent.
- Blue-collar
  - Disadvantages
    - Again, some of the tenants might not be financially responsible, so it may be unconvincing to threaten them with eviction or dinging their credit.

- Will take more effort to screen and select ideal tenants.
- May consider Section 8 tenants for full occupancy.
  o Advantages
    - Usually very committed to paying rent as first bill every month
    - Very employable, when " pink – slipped" can find another local job soon
    - Capable of own maintenance and upgrades
- Upscale
  o Advantages
    - Often sees the best short-term appreciation in real estate values.
    - Financially responsible tenants, so should see timely rents.
  o Disadvantages
    - Tenants may be quite demanding, requesting upgrades for their own taste.
    - Mortgage payment and other costs may be relatively higher compared to the rent, so ratio of rent/ PITIMM could reduce profit.
    - Section 8 tenants would not be welcome, as it could ruin local culture, so not an alternative.

With low interest rates and a booming real estate market currently, foreclosures are more rare, and your next investment property will probably have to be bought on the open market through a real estate agent. Sure, you'd like to avoid paying the 4 to 6 percent commission, but often that's the only way to obtain the best property. Prudent sellers know they can demand the best possible price with full exposure in an open market.

In times where foreclosures were more common than today, some banks maintained a real estate owned (REO) list of houses the bank has repossessed through the foreclosure process. It may take a few emails or a few phone calls, but you can get to the REO manager or REO list at a bank that is actively lending in your area. From there, you can make an offer on the house or property of interest. Actually, more often, you're required to pay the bank's already bargain price.

Weed through this list, and you may determine that this is one of those rare occasions where you can make money by flipping a house. If you're lucky, you may find one or two properties on the list that you may want to keep long-term as rentals. Often, the banks want to get these properties off their books quickly and will require you to go elsewhere for financing.

I've had some success with REO lists. I have two rentals obtained in this manner. However, I went back to the known REO manager for this bank active in the IE, and he informed me that they were no longer maintaining a list. Instead, they had a selected an REO broker, and I should contact him. I didn't bother, as once exposed to the open market, these are no longer a bargain.

Different banks have different policies for REOs, and these policies tend to change. I mention banks' REO lists as a possible way to acquire property at a bargain price. Of course, review carefully to assure adequate condition of the property, as banks sell off this list in as-is condition and rarely upgrade. However, you can be assured of clean title, as the foreclosure process cleanses minor liens.

During my MBA coursework at Cal State Fullerton, Professor Collins in Finance credited me with coining the acronym PITIMM to assess cash flow: principal, interest, taxes, insurance, maintenance (including upgrades), and management. I feel the need to properly assess cash flow, as it is the bottom line in real estate investing on a month-to-month basis. Further, most of the books I had read on real estate investing talked about the mortgage payment, which is principal and interest, and assumed that these versus the rent yield cash flow. This is simply not true, as many new investors have learned the hard way. These other four factors can be significant. More than a few real estate investors have thought they were in cash-positive cash flow only to be blindsided by a hefty annual property tax invoice and/or special tax assessment.

Other factors of PITIMM can vary and negatively impact cash

flow. While the mortgage and interest payments are usually a constant based on the mortgage you've obtained, many of the other PITIMM factors are negotiable. Yes, even property tax, as I have challenged tax assessments and had some success in lowering property tax. Contact the tax assessor in your county to learn the procedure, which usually requires comps (similar comparable properties).

Go online to shop insurance brokers and obtain the best rate. Rarely is it one of the major known players in the insurance business but a smaller company specializing in non-owner-occupied investment property. However, carefully evaluate before you file a claim, as after paying the deductible, the amount you gain from the claim may soon be insignificant when rates are increased on all your income properties.

Insurance companies are looking to make a profit, and they don't want to pay claims. Your claims are on record, so changing insurance carriers to avoid a rate hike probably won't work. Every mortgage lender I know requires insurance, and you must provide this information annually to your lender.

The only insurance claim I remember filing was to replace a house that was torched when a firestorm swept through San Bernardino. Claim was paid in full, plus lost rents, and I used the proceeds as down payments on two houses. In this case, my claim was one of hundreds of claims and expected by the insurance carriers, so I was not extraordinary as an investor filing a claim.

Management costs vary with the number of properties you have with the property management service, the services they provide, and your level of participation. I pay zero for most of my properties, as I manage myself. I use Propman to manage some of my houses, and they do an excellent job.

The going rate is 50 percent of the first month's rent to repay the management service for selecting, clearing, and placing the best tenant. From there, if the management service continues to collect the rent, they will usually charge 6 percent of the rent payment each month. On occasion, with a tenant in arrears, I will ask my handyman to visit the property, arrange a pre-payment plan, and collect the past-due rent. He charges 8 percent for this service.

Maintenance charges certainly vary. We usually repaint the interior when a tenant moves out. With houses, this is often seven years or more. Often, the tenant will make a specific upgrade request—painting, landscaping, flooring, etc. We will respond to the request and complete the work if we feel it's mutually beneficial to improve the property and keep the tenant satisfied. On many occasions, I make this offer: I will pay for materials if you, the tenant, provide the labor. Usually that's a win-win situation. We are always looking to upgrade the property and justify rent increases.

Getting even more geographically specific, I will always walk the neighborhood and talk to neighbors before I finalize an offer. I remember making an offer on a house in Riverside, California, one evening. I was wary that I just didn't know enough about the neighborhood, so I came back the next day about four thirty in the afternoon and just wandered around to talk to any available neighbors.

A very pleasant lady tending her garden responded when I ask about the neighborhood with the question, "Do you like getting up at five thirty every morning?"

I laughed and said, "No, almost never."

She then responded, "Oh, then that's not the house for you, because the train comes rumbling through, if you look about a hundred feet behind your house, and it's about five on the Richter scale and very loud. No one on that side of the street can sleep through it."

So an investment house that appeared to be bargain wasn't, and had I bought this house, I would have had constant turnover—a landlord's worst enemy.

My neighborhood walks have provided other interesting results. In one instance, a woman told me her daughter, son-in-law, and granddaughter were looking at moving out of her house, and it would be wonderful if they could move into my place right across the street. She said she would guarantee the rent if they couldn't. So I made a neighborhood friend and still have an excellent tenant five years later.

Sure, on other occasions, I have had to listen to much useless neighborhood gossip. But ultimately, I usually obtain some valuable info. Never forget the neighborhood walk and talk before you invest.

So, back to my peers in the MBA finance class. They were quite encouraging, had some pertinent questions, but overall were very endorsing that we had started off with a great deal getting these twelve houses together at a bargain price. Some students with more experience than I in mortgages did have some prudent advice. But most of my peers had only a sprinkling of experience in real estate investing, often through a family member. Macroeconomics were quite favorable then, as nationwide real estate values were rebounding, especially in the west, based on recently lowered interest rates.

Unfortunately, these endorsements went to my head, leading to my first mistake. See chapter 13 on inevitable downturns.

Calculating Multiunit Variations

The fair price of a multiunit building is sometimes more difficult to calculate. A common term is the gross rent multiplier (GRM), a metric utilized to quickly calculate a property's profitability compared to similar properties within the same real estate market. To determine the GRM, you would divide the price of the property by its gross rental income. A good gross multiplier depends heavily on the type of rental market in which your property exists. Normally, you want to achieve a goal of a GRM between four and seven. A lower GRM means it will take less time to pay off your rental property.

Ron, who runs his family trust, a real estate investment, comments: "Looking at the gross multiplier, the real estate agent convinced me this eight-unit apartment building in Long Beach was our best investment. A year later, I was trying to figure out how he did his accounting, as even lowering our standards for tenants, we could not keep reliable tenants staying and paying. Yes, I felt deceived. Perhaps it was a change in the area, lowering overall standards. Probably not our best investment, as we were in the red for the first couple of years."

When to Buy

Mortgage rates dip

Cooling inflation and slower global economic growth led mortgage rates this week to their lowest levels in a year

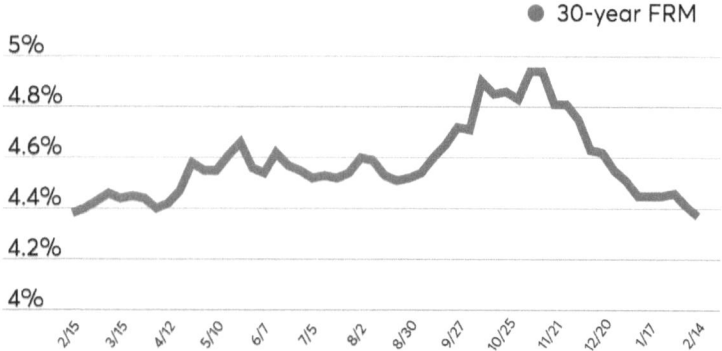

Source: Freddie Mac https://www.freddiemac.com/pmms

And finally on this topic, when should we be buying property? This graph from Freddie Mac shows seasonal fluctuations in interest rates. As expected, the late-year holidays and the usual school year lead to less lending activity and hence lower interest rates and mortgage interest rates from November through February, then increasing with the summer buying season. Shopping for investment property in the off-season—November through February—can be somewhat of a double-edged sword, as we can secure lower interest rates on our mortgages but inventory may also be down. If you find an adequate property, the seller may be desperate to try to unload off-season, so you can negotiate.

I've had the best success in buying at under-market prices during the off-season. Typically, I have a few real estate agents with a successful track record in the IE who are aware of my plans, and they keep an eye out for me for an ideal property in the off-season that might become available.

Another seasonal change we notice is that property values seem to show the sharpest spike when the buying season starts in the spring. So what may not appear to be a bargain in January or February may turn out to be a bargain by the spring buying season, as the value of your newly acquired property spikes.

CHAPTER 2

Negotiating the Purchase Price

Most factors of real estate investing are negotiable, and the purchase price is often the most negotiable. There are many issues to be considered here. Are we currently in a strong real estate market where sellers usually get at or near their price? Is it a weaker market where sellers are anxious for any offer? There certainly is seasonality to real estate purchasing, as in the winter months, perhaps starting in November through February, there is less real estate activity (see Graph 1).

There is also a seasonality to interest rates, as the rates are usually somewhat lower in these slower real estate sales months. Winter is often my favorite time to be buying real estate, as there are fewer buyers to compete with, and the sellers will be somewhat desperate. Again, less inventory during these slower months could limit property choices. Don't be too selective, as you are not planning to live there, and your prospective tenant is probably more tolerant.

FOSBO or Listed Property ?

How did you find the property for sale? Is it listed on the open market, or perhaps you directly contacted the owner? Maybe it is a for sale by owner (FoSBO), just a sign on the lawn and an email address. That was a tactic we would often use, perhaps driving through a neighborhood near where we already had a house and looking for a perhaps vacant house or one in poor condition. Hopefully, it was a house with a desperate owner, or perhaps the property was bank-owned. In either case, there was someone who would welcome an offer. We were always in a position where we had handyman help to upgrade a fixer-upper, but of course it had to be reflected in the price, and we would negotiate for the lowest possible price.

Fixer-upper is a vague, overused term in the real estate business. Note that according to many savvy real estate agents, it attracts more attention, as potential buyers want to believe they will find a bargain. Splash on some paint and a few bushes on the property, increase the price by 25 percent, and flip it, or so they think.

In fact, I have one real estate agent who routinely uses this phrase to gain more contacts of potential buyers. Karen, a top-producing real estate agent in the IE, says she puts *fixer-upper* in the listing on any house that might have some deferred maintenance. It helps her sell this property, plus gains her additional potential buyers.

Just be aware: Is the status of fixer-upper reflected in the price? Will the repairs exceed your proposed budget?

Let me back up a step. So you see a house or maybe a small apartment building that looks in disrepair, maybe vacant, and you want to contact the owner. Never hurts to knock on the door and talk to the tenant or the owner to get started. Maybe leave a note. If there's no response in either case, go to your title company for that county and ask for a property profile, title search, or whatever other terminology their customer service uses. You can learn a great deal from this title search, such as what loans or liens are against the property, what it previously sold for and when, and of course, owner information. Contact the owner to discuss details and a possible purchase.

Your intent in all these procedures is to avoid paying a 4 to 6 percent commission to the real estate agent, and maybe get a bargain price before an agent escalates the price. However, this is not always rewarded, as some sellers have outlandish ideas about the value of their property.

Once in contact with the owner, I never trash or say demeaning things about the property. Why insult the seller unnecessarily? In fact, I usually go the other way and find a reason to compliment the property and say I wouldn't be here if I wasn't interested. I have studied negotiating in all aspects of my businesses, and maintaining a pleasant relationship with the opposing party is always recommended.

Lower Price ?

So how do I go about offering a lower price than what the seller wants? Earlier in my real estate career (phase 1), I could get away with making the statement, "That's all I can afford." As Delinco got better known in the IE, everyone knew I could pay anything I wanted. So my tactic was slightly different. I would say, "I'm looking at your house, and I have several other houses I am making offers on today." That's usually a true statement. "I favor your property, but I need to buy it at this price to work for our plans."

Other typical negotiating tactics sometimes apply and will benefit. A key tool that most investors don't realize they can offer is a prequalification letter. So you have a lender that has financed many of your transactions and is ready to finance more. Once you provide current financials, have the lender issue a letter saying that you are prequalified. So you make an offer to the seller, another buyer makes an offer, perhaps at an even higher price, but that offer is contingent on sale of their existing residence. The seller will inevitably favor your offer with the prequalification letter and without the contingency.

Inspection by building engineer

The next interesting tactic is the use of a structural or building engineer. For a fee, you can hire this engineer to inspect a property with the owner's cooperation. I don't often sell properties—I'm usually looking to buy and hold long-term—but other conditions have sometimes changed that strategy (such as divorce). So in one instance, when I was selling a property, this tactic was first used on me.

The buyer said he favored my house but was naïve about the

construction and condition of HVAC, water heater, plumbing, etc., so he wanted to hire a structural engineer or building engineer (I think the latter; the two occupations are closely related). Anyway, a building engineer worth his credentials can find at least $8,000 and more likely $15,000 worth of possible upgrades needed for the house. So this building engineer inspected my house, which was basically in good condition, and found $9,000 worth of possible upgrades.

You probably guess what happened next. The buyer used the building report to negotiate a better price. He said he would split the difference with me and reduced his offer by $4,500. We negotiated further, but I did have to lower my price, as it was a weak real estate market and I did not have a back-up buyer at that time.

Next time somebody tried that tactic, I, of course, had to cooperate and allow him to inspect the house, but I told him I didn't want to see the report. He insisted on showing it to me and I said, "Sure, email it, I have a delete key on my PC" and reiterated that I did not want to see the report and would not consider it in any negotiation. He then backed off paying for the building inspection and paid our agreed price. We both knew that the house was in good condition and a building report was unnecessary.

In several cases, I have had to use a building engineer to inspect the property when I recognized it had been neglected and was afraid the condition could be worse than expected. And yes, I did use the report to negotiate a better price. So it's a possible negotiating tactic, but whether or not you intend to use this tactic, it is certainly one you should be aware of. Sometimes such a building report is a necessity to fully evaluate your potential maintenance costs, per the stated intent.

Once, I did violate my usual policy of complimenting the property to the seller, as my competitor and sometimes colleague, Ken, had made an offer on a Fontana property and insisted the seller was unreasonable on his price. Admittedly a tactic of questionable ethics. I visited the house; toured carefully with the seller, noting every possible problem; then made an offer $10,000 under Ken's offer. This was Ken's request of me, and he promised he would reciprocate when I needed him.

I wasn't in a buying mode and expected my offer to be quickly rejected. It was. I think the buyer softened a bit, but Ken did finally buy this house. I never asked him to reciprocate, and fortunately, he did not make this request of me again. I want to be recognized as ethical and stand behind any offer I make.

Title Search

Knowledge is power. Once you have the title search, you may find some interesting information. One property I was buying had a small lien on it from a plumber. When negotiating with the seller, I mentioned this lien and suggested there could be more liens. I told him I would do him a big favor and accept the property as-is and would take responsible for paying off his liens.

He was feisty and didn't think he owed the money to the plumber, but his wife was more cooperative, and they accepted my offer. So I paid the plumber his due, plus the requisite 10 percent, and the lien was removed for less than $1,000. I bought the house for about $12,000 under market.

Other important information can be presented in a title search. In one case, some clown was trying to sell a property that was in a family trust, without his siblings' knowledge. My experienced escrow lady warned that the legal wrangling could last years. I did not make an offer.

Every adequate real estate agent has completed the title search before listing the property. It's a fairly obvious step, as she can't get paid if escrow can't close.

Often FoSBO—specifically *for sale by owner* houses—can offer you as the investor a lower price, as the 6 or 4 percent commission is not required. That's certainly an advantage for the seller. Do note that you are now fully responsible for all aspects of the property, so title search and maybe even an inspection by a property engineer could be prudent.

Selling a property

On the rare occasions when I sell a property, I always list through the multiple listing service and select one of the top-producing local real estate agents. In this way, my property is exposed to the full market, and I believe I'm getting maximum fair price. Usually, you should expect to pay 6 percent commission to the real estate agents—listing and selling—usually split evenly. Lower commission usually means the property is of higher value, maybe 4 percent if the property is selling for over $1 million. This is negotiable.

Sometimes, before I list the property, I will negotiate a lower commission with the understanding that I am going to do most of the work needed for selling, and the agent's effort will be less. Certainly I am more knowledgeable, so it will take less of their time to complete the sale. Also on more than a few occasions, when I am evaluating an offer lower than expected, I will respond by saying "Yes, I'll accept this offer if you will knock 1 percent off your commission rate."

When buying an investment property, your negotiating position is always improved if you can find a property on your own, rather than having a buyer's agent find it and present it to you. Real estate agents split commissions, so if there is no buyer's agent, chances are you can successfully ask the listing agent to reduce commission by a percent or two. The net commission for the listing agent is still greater than the usual 50-50 split with the buyer's agent.

However, depending on how familiar you are with your investment area, it can be useful to have a local agent aware of your ideal property. With an active market, you may need to respond quickly to buy your ideal investment property, in which case your local agent earns that commission. Be ready respond appropriately, as these dynamics vary.

Multi – Unit properties

Regarding apartment buildings: I've seen many different ways of presenting this prevalent gross multiplier information from various real estate agents. I remember we were shopping for apartment buildings in the Inglewood area, and the agents would always show an excellent GRM. Of course, too often listing agents will base their GRM on 100 percent occupancy, while in Inglewood, under the LAX flight path, turnover was too common and 100 percent occupancy an unrealistic pipe dream.

Prudent investors will learn the market, shop for a while, walk and talk, and discuss with multiple real estate agents before making an offer. Often the listing agent will not include utilities, repairs, upgrades, etc., leaving a distorted, overly optimistic assessment. An investor certainly should request this information, as the GRM ratio does not include these very pertinent expenses

Sound confusing? It is, even more so when an experienced real estate broker purposely tries to deceive the naïve first-time apartment-building buyer. There are many ways to misconstrue the facts and leave out key detrimental factors, with the incentive of a large commission.

Most new buyers of multiunit buildings have commented that they were disappointed with their first purchase. They paid too much for it, didn't fully recognize what they were buying, didn't realize some other negative factors about the building, expenses were underrepresented, etc.

CHAPTER 3

Financing

Including an Interview with Marty Prince, Mortgage Technology

Other People's Money

The term I've seen often in real estate investing books is OPM—other people's money, or money borrowed from a bank or other lender. Ideally, you want to make a down payment of 10 percent and then finance the remaining 90 percent. However, more commonly, for non-owner-occupied property, 20 percent down is required.

Here's an example of the benefit of OPM in real estate investing: Dear Uncle George has passed and left you a $100,000 inheritance. You decide to buy an apartment building for $500,000. Using the $100,000 as a down payment, you take out a loan for $400,000. You've invested well, and the apartment building increases in value by 20 percent in the next year, so now it's worth $600,000. Using OPM, you have doubled your money, with your equity now at $200,000.

Contrarily, maybe you want to invest the full $100,000 in the stock market. You've selected well—a blue-chip stock—and again seen an increase of 20 percent in one year. Your investment is now worth $120,000.

The established principal of OPM in real estate investment allows you to control more with your invested money. *Leverage* is the common term. My examples are oversimplifications, to be sure, but they show the principle of leverage—controlling more with a down payment and borrowed money, OPM.

Another factor to be considered is the benefit of liquidity, as it takes me four keystrokes and one day to take cash out of my Schwab account, while selling or borrowing against real estate is time-consuming and can be expensive. In fact, most real estate transactions involve commissions, loan fees, escrow fees—estimates are 6 to 10 percent of the transaction. Adding complexity to this comparison, per the title of this book, real estate investments can offer a significant tax shelter.

Credit

To use other people's money, you have to maintain good credit so they can be assured you will repay on time. As a real estate investor and property owner, you may be much more vulnerable than you might believe to unfair credit dings. If you are already an investment property owner, there may already be unpleasant credit surprises waiting for you.

You may know that utility services, including trash disposal, can ding your credit as the owner of a property with an unpaid invoice from one of your tenants. Specifically, a lien is recorded against the property with you as owner. In addition to forcing you to eventually pay this utility bill, in some counties the utility bill is added to your next year's property tax invoice.

Too many agencies see us investors as "deep pockets," and we need to oppose this when possible. I often present overdue utility bills to the tenants, requiring them to pay and provide proof. If a tenant is negligent in these duties and has moved on, of course I'm stuck paying the bill, but the sooner the better to protect my credit.

Credit issues for investors can get worse from there. I remember asking a local plumbing service for an estimate on a major project. The estimate was presented, but my handyman said he could get a partner and do the job for half that estimate. Always wanting to keep my handyman employed and paid, I went that route, and the project was completed.

A year later, when routinely checking my credit, I noticed this plumbing company—I think they were called Dewey, Cheatham, and Howe—had claimed they completed the work and I had not paid for it. Subsequently, DC&H plumbers were demanding payment by placing a lien on the property. A mechanics lien such as this is certainly recognized by the courts and has to be addressed.

I paid for good legal advice, then went to court pro per. The plumbing company was conveniently unrepresented, so I was able to easily get the baseless lien removed. Take this as a warning about sleazy contractors. I should have checked Yelp and other reviews on this, and any contractor, before even contacting them.

Next, let's say you're suffering a downturn in your area and you find you are stuck with too many alligators—that is, negative-cash-flow properties—and not enough funds in reserve to cover all mortgages and other monthly expenses. There are several solutions here: you can borrow money to maintain the mortgage payments and the properties, or you can punt and give up one or two of the alligators.

Sometimes, if you're behind on payments, the lender will accept a deed in lieu of foreclosure. This deed in lieu does reduce their legal bills and gets them control of the property sooner. It also shows you are willing to work with the lender through this problem. However, some lenders see the foreclosure process as a cleansing process, as all other minor liens are necessarily removed. Hence, some lenders won't accept a deed in lieu; instead, they will proceed with the full foreclosure procedure.

So you'd like to invest in real estate, but you've gotten yourself in a little bit of credit trouble? You'll be pleasantly surprised by what credit services can accomplish these days. You may want to write your own letters to the creditors, but I have worked through various credit services over the years. Most recently, Lexington Law has been very helpful in getting false, and even some marginally deserved, credit dings removed.

Your first step may be to check your own credit. Respond as needed from there to assure the highest FICO rating. Marty Prince, owner of Mortgage Technology, offers this information:

> A top-tier mortgage applicant would be FICO score of 740 or above. Below that, you fall to second, third, or fourth tier, dropping a tier every 20 points on your FICO score. Each drop in tier adds about 1/8 %. (Currently, there are more considerations or loan requirements than just FICO scores, as the real estate crash of 2008 has added more banking restrictions.)
>
> For example, say a top-tier borrower buys an investment house with 20 percent down and a loan of $400,000 at the best interest rate of 5.875 percent, (term of thirty years. Monthly payment is $2,366. A second- or third-tier borrower, would have to pay 6.5 percent or more, one percentage point higher, so the monthly payment with a thirty-year term is $2,528.

Over the first ten years of the loan, the payment difference is about $20,000 to the disfavor of the second-tier borrower. For a shorter term loan, the payment difference would be less.

> It's certainly worth the effort to achieve and maintain a top-tier credit rating. Considering accurate monthly cash flow assessment using PITIMM, the mortgage payment is usually the major factor. It's worth the effort to minimize the mortgage payment.
>
> When buying an apartment building, you can claim owner-occupied if the building is four units or less, and get the best interest rate (assuming, of course, that you do live in this apartment building). More than four units—say you're buying an eight-unit apartment building—and you can't claim owner-occupied. Even with an excellent top-tier FICO score, you would pay almost one percentage point more with

non-owner-occupied financing, the only financing available for the larger unit buildings.

For example, today the best interest rate with an excellent FICO score would be about 5.5 percent for an owner-occupied mortgage loan on a residence. If the same borrower were buying an eight-unit apartment building, owner-occupied or not, the interest rate would be about 6.5 percent. (OK, if you are rich enough to buy an eight-unit apartment building, you probably have a lovely residence in upper suburbia.)

Thanks, Marty.

Appraisal

Any property being financed is subject to an appraisal. Most real estate investors think this is just another step, and often it is of little relevance. However, there can be occasions where you might need a lower appraisal to convince sellers that their property isn't worth quite what they are expecting. Or you might need a higher appraisal to qualify for a loan.

We all assume that the appraiser works totally independently and draws his own conclusion. While this is often true, on more than a few occasions I've been able to influence the appraiser in the direction needed. I remember one house where we needed a higher appraisal than what would normally be expected, as prices had risen quickly—so I did the appraiser's job for him. I went through a series of probably forty comparable properties and came up with the three I thought were close enough to the property of interest and in the price range I needed. When the appraiser came to visit the properties, I left these three comps printed out there. Remember, I was paying him, so he did need to listen to me regardless. Usually, appraisers will appreciate it if you do their job for them and provide the comps, as ultimately, that is where they get the final amount of the appraisal. Further, I did call this appraiser to add my local "expertise" to his decision process.

When possible, I'd like to meet appraisers at the property. This way, I can pay them by check, and they see that I am a real estate investment business and not just an individual, and thus a source of future business. This also gives me occasion to present the comps without any paper trail. If not possible, of course, I email the selected comps, but this can be a problem, as there is now a paper trail.

In any case, I usually tell the appraiser in so many words the expected value and have the comps to justify this number. "Again, Mr. or Ms. Appraiser, these are the properties that I have reviewed and are closest to subject property in square footage, lot size, condition, geographic area, etc." Full justification of the comps you want used is needed, and why other comps are irrelevant. Anyone can find comps from a variety of recognized real estate sources with a few keystrokes, so more explanation is required for the desired appraisal amount.

Note that with Zillow, Trulia, Redfin, and other real estate sources available with a few keystrokes, convincing your appraiser to vary greatly from these posted values is more of a challenge. It may be safest to request and justify smaller variances. Anyway, I've usually been able to get close to the appraisal value required by doing the appraiser's homework for him.

Currently, the Fed promises continuing interest rate increases to combat inflation, which is the usual response to rapid inflation. However, to the real estate investor's benefit, the current inflation trend does include property values and rents. In most areas, these property increases are significantly greater than interest rate increases.

CHAPTER 4

Selecting Tenants

Including an Interview with Kerry Spelman, Propman

Consistent with the usual goal of minimizing costs, I self-manage most of my houses. However, about ten years ago, I found I was having problems with my own minimal screening procedure, so I reviewed available property management services in the IE. After one disastrous selection (see chapter 8, "Anecdotes," for my story about the property manager from hell), I offered three houses to Kerry of Propman.

In the following Q and A interview, she shares some of her procedures:

Q: Kerry, what is your initial procedure in screening prospective new tenants?

A: We check all social media, contact previous landlords, verify income, pull credit. We also use a system that runs background checks that goes beyond the five years (that is a proprietary). We also try to see where they live now and look in their cars. Often times, how they treat their car is how they will treat the rental.

Q: I've had the worst experiences with teenage boys who graffiti walls and vandalize. What is your worst damage experience?

A: The most damage I have seen is from a small dog that peed everywhere, and the carpet and cement had to be replaced and steamed. As long as we screen really well, I usually do not have any problems.

Q: Do you ever attempt cash for keys?

A: Yes, we always try mediation first—depending on how much they owe, cash for keys works.

Q: When needed, how long do evictions take?

A: These days, evictions could take up to four to five months, the courts are completely backlogged and lockouts are taking up to two months for the same reason.

Q: How long do most tenants stay in the same unit ?

A: Most tenants stay two to three years. I have had good luck with both houses and apartments.

Thanks, Kerry.

Most experienced landlords and property management services will attempt to negotiate a tenant out of a property before initiating the full five- or six-month eviction process with money judgment. What you are offering the tenant is no negative credit rating, no money judgment against their credit, no further credit ding, and all they have to do is leave you a somewhat clean house, give you the keys, and agree to vacate.

My cash for keys letter is very simple:

> ### Agreement and receipt
>
> Tenant John Q Deadbeat agrees to completely vacate the house located at 111 W. 1ˢᵗ St., Anytown, CA, 99999 on 31 February, 2022, for payment of $1,000 from the landlord and owner Daryl Deliman.
>
> Agreed, receipt John Q. Deadbeat_____
> Date_____

(Note that this agreement was not written by an attorney, nor advised by an attorney, nor has it been tested in any legal proceeding. It's never been challenged and has always worked for its purpose.)

I usually have the tenant outside the property when the agreement and receipt are signed, and I write the tenant a check rather than give cash, just in case there is an unpleasant surprise within the house or the property, and I need to stop payment on the check. Also, while this transaction is ongoing, my handyman or a locksmith is changing all of the locks.

Finally, while I always have a second copy of this agreement for tenants hidden in my notebook, I never offer a copy unless they demand a copy. Usually, they are too focused on my check to request a copy of this agreement. I'm sure somehow it could be used against me.

Kerry suggests that she has not been seriously deceived by any prospective tenants, possibly because her procedure is a bit more stringent. Other property managers mention being victims of identity theft. This other property manager later observed money orders coming in a different name and investigated further to confirm the identify theft. Another property manager complained that a prospective tenant somehow managed to get several very negative, but legitimate, dings removed from his credit record.

CHAPTER 5

Care and Feeding of Tenants

For landlords, good tenants are the lifeblood of our business. A tenant who stays and pays and takes care of the property can make us successful. In contrast, a very bad tenant can be the bane of our existence, and the potential for damage is almost limitless.

Shari was a real estate contact of my brother Dennis's, with years of experience in property management as well as real estate in general. We hired her to get us started when we bought the twelve HUD houses. I remember overhearing a phone conversation she had with delinquent tenant:

"Delinco Properties is not family, not your friend, and especially not a bank. You are living in a Delinco house and have a business contract with Delinco Properties. Please live up to your end of the contract. After you put food on the table, the next item you pay is the rent, to keep a roof over your family's head." From there I learned to maintain a businesslike relationship of mutual respect with tenants.

Contrast that with another friend who dabbled in real estate investment and later got out. "It'd be great to own rental properties," this friend had said. "When needed, I can help out a friend or family member with a place to stay."

So what's wrong with renting to friends and family? Sooner usually rather than later, there will be an issue about rent being late or care of the property. With friends, this could end up as a chapter in how to lose friends and alienate people quickly. With family, you'll end up the pariah of the family, as they don't expect you to evict or complain about a family member being trashy in your property or failing to pay.

Note that in many states and counties, if someone spends the night and has a toothbrush in your bathroom, or accepts mail at your residence, you may have to legally evict. Hence, even a supposed temporary stay can turn ugly.

I try to maintain a professional relationship with tenants, one of mutual respect, as we landlords need tenants who take care of the property and pay the rent on time. I try to remain somewhat aloof, as I don't want to be seen as an indulging friend. I think it is important that as landlords and owners, we show a constant interest in the property to make sure the tenant is maintaining it. I do this in many ways, and most of my tenants know me by sight.

Understanding Tenant Contracts

An important first step in the landlord–tenant relationship in the contract. A broad variety of monthly rental or annual lease contracts are available online. Or, if you're working with a property manager, they have probably selected their ideal lease contract.

Tenants sometimes feel more secure if they have a yearly lease contract at an agreed rent as opposed to month-to-month. As a landlord, I really don't see much disadvantage to a yearly lease contract, as I certainly want my tenants to stay as long as possible, assuming they take care of the property and pay the rent on time. This assumes your are intending on keeping the property longterm, note if you intend to sell this or next year, month to month lease is best

Most rental contracts have all the standard information and requirements. But there are four important items that are not always on standard rental contracts that I always make sure are in any rental contract on my properties:

1. Late fee (of $80 or more) due after the tenth of the month. There are various legal requirements and certainly a

maximum that you can charge for late fee, which can vary county to county or state to state. Often about 8 percent on the monthly rent is the maximum. Also, if you ask for a money judgment, the late fee usually cannot be included as part of the money judgment even if you have it in the contract.

2. The tenant is responsible for paying all utility bills on time. Owner is copied almost always now, so when you receive a late utility bill, you can present it to the tenant and require immediate payment. Perhaps they write the check, and you send it into the utility. If the tenant skips out and the utility bill is still due, the property owner will have to pay it. Many counties allow the utility company to add the overdue bill to the next year's property tax.

3. Who occupies the property, by name—how many people and/or pets. Any visitors can stay only three days. Rent will be increased if visitors remain more than three days.

4. The tenant must keep the house and the yard in good condition, and the landlord has the right to visit and inspect inside the house with twenty-four-hour notice. (I rarely use the visit clause. It is usually considered very antagonistic, but it's important just as a warning that you maintain that right so they should take care of the property.)

Raising the Rent

We got into this business to make money, so it's usually negligent not to have an annual rent increase. However, we do have to study the current economy and other factors before raising the rent. I usually try to keep my rent increases under $100 or 7 percent per year, as that doesn't sting quite as much for the tenants. But sometimes this just isn't enough. The key aspect here is we don't want to increase the rent so much that the tenant will want, or be forced, to leave.

As a landlord, turnover is usually your biggest enemy, as you're going to lose a couple month's rent and need to upgrade the house from one tenant to the next. Hence, the total cost on a house is usually about $7,000, on an apartment about $3,800.

See below for my rent increase notice. Notice how I referred to a recognized source, in this case Zillow, to justify the rent increase and confirm that our rents are still below the average for the area. Also, as further justification, I've usually done some work on every house every year. And I accept rents after the tenth of the month without forcing late fees.

Usually, I get little blowback from rent increases. People expect them, as we all tolerate inflation. Also note, I am apologetic about costs increasing, and express that I hope this isn't a burden to them or their family. Again, as landlords, we need good tenants who will stay, pay on time, and not demand unnecessary upgrades.

A typical rent increase letter, with elements listed above:

> Mr. and Mrs. Renter
> Riverside, CA
> RE: Rent increase
> Dear Mr. and Ms. Renter,
>
> Many of our expenses have increased this year, such as taxes, insurance, mortgage payments, and maintenance costs. Also, we have done upgrades and maintenance work on your house. Finally, you have been occasionally late with the rent and have not included the late fee.
>
> Hence, we are increasing the rent. Starting March 1, in 85 days, the rent will be $2,500 per month. Notice this is still less than the county average for a three-bedroom two-bath home with two-car garage, as the county average is $2,800 per month. Zillow gives an estimated rent of $2,900 per month.

We appreciate your continued tenancy and hope this is not too great a burden for the Renter family.

Sincerely,
Daryl Deliman
Delinco owner
cc: Delinco accountant

Perhaps a benefit of turnover is that a greater rent increase is then possible. Usually when a tenant moves out, we will compare local rents and increase appropriately. With a new tenant, I can increase rents by $200 to $300, or 15 percent, assuming the market will bear it. I understand this is the only case where you can raise rents as much as needed in rent-controlled areas.

On other occasions, when perhaps the economy of the area, or the country, has gone temporarily south, I do avoid increasing rents. When needed, I work with tenants on payment plans that will keep them in the house. There's not much else I can offer, as it is important that I collect the total rent for each house every month.

Realistically, it's not always possible. If someone has lost a job or there is some other family downturn, I will offer some relief. If they are an established tenant with an acceptable payment record, I will waive one, possibly two months' full or partial rent. I try to get them to pay at least partial rent every month. Sometimes we have a written repayment plan with the tenant. Further, I warn the tenant I can offer a waiver only once.

My dialogue: "Dear Mr. or Ms. Tenant, I am a businessperson and have partners and an accountant who insist on a full month's rent every month. So I emphasize that this is a one-time waiver, and if such a problem happens again, you should plan on moving, as I'll be forced to evict, and that can negatively affect your credit."

Paying the Rent

If your investment property is in an upscale area, and your tenants have bank accounts and are computer savvy, they can certainly directly transfer the rent money every month into your account. Many banks have specific online banking services. I use Bank of America, and they have Zelle, where tenants can directly pay me. Also using Zelle, I pay my handyman and other contractors.

As mentioned, IE is more of what I would refer to as a blue-collar area. Most of my tenants have checking accounts, but some have lost that privilege due to financial problems and bouncing too many checks. With most banking apps today, I can accept and use the banking app to deposit a personal check, cashiers checks, and some money orders. However, most money orders have to be deposited at the bank.

Many tenants still pay me via standard mail. On the contract, it says the payment must be received by the tenth of the month or there is a late fee of approximately 5 percent, stated specifically in the contract as $80. I'm sure there's a legal limit in most areas; on the late fee. I think it's 8 percent.

In earlier years, too often I would hear the excuse, "Well, I sent the rent on the sixth, it must be lost in the mail," or "I'm glad you called, I didn't have your address so I haven't sent the rent yet." I have a great deal more confidence in the US mail than the credibility of many of my tenants.

My solution to that problem was very easy. I went to a printer and requested addressed envelopes in a unique color. I chose green, as I usually receive very few green-colored envelopes in the mail. Between my visits and handyman visits, I make sure all tenants have many addressed green envelopes, so I rarely have to hear the excuse, "I didn't have your address" or "I sent it, it must've been lost in the mail." The distinctive green envelopes make that already flimsy excuse even less plausible.

On the few houses that I have through a property manager, Propman collects the rent, and it is directly deposited into my account after they take their 6 percent.

Eviction

Sometimes, a legal eviction with money judgment against a tenant is necessary. Note that the money judgement can belong to the property manager or the property owner, depending on how the legal action is filed. On filing evictions, your best path might be determined by the area in which you have selected to invest. If it is an upscale area, chances are with today's computerized credit services, your money judgment will eventually be paid, plus the requisite 10 percent. If you're in a blue-collar or semi-slum area, chances are slim that you will have any money judgment repaid.

Hence, in filing evictions, I usually ask for possession of the property only, so the tenant won't contest the eviction. In this manner, we usually get possession of the property sooner. If the action notifies the tenant that the owner wants possession only, they will want to stay as long as possible for free, but will move out without attending court to contest. When a money judgement is demanded, there's a much better chance the tenant will appear to contest the amount owed.

If the tenant does insist on contesting, I upgrade the action and ask for a money judgment, which usually changes the tenant's mind to contest. When possible, it's best to discuss these issues by phone with the tenant, maybe via a third party, rather than by expensive and time-consuming legal means.

If you have been a landlord for long enough, you will succeed in legal evictions and win money judgements. There are services that will collect or attempt to collect on money judgments on your behalf. I was contacted by one of these services, and the gentleman said that after he inspects the validity of my money judgments, he will buy them from me based on fifty cents on the dollar

Not too encouraging, and if I were totally in an upscale area, I would not consider his offer but instead wait to collect the full amount with the usual 10 percent interest. However, in a blue-collar area, considering 100 percent of zero is still zero, I will work with him when possible. He reviewed the series of I think twelve money judgments I had. He was less than encouraging, as he noted several of my evicted tenants also had

IRS liens, and his very valid comment was, "If the IRS can't collect on these money judgements, I'm sure I can't either."

So I sold him a few of my money judgments where he expressed interest. This collection service did note that a money judgement is often a powerful tool, as it is difficult to rent another unit with that credit ding. In retrospect, from my experience, I'm better off forgetting asking for a money judgment and just getting immediate possession of the property. There will be fewer months of lost rent, possible extended damage, or even vandalism to the house. A tenant angry with the landlord can be destructive.

Pets

I've always been a dog lover, and I'm also fond of cats. So I feel it would be hypocritical for me to attempt to ban pets from my houses. Also, in some neighborhoods of Inland Empire, a dog may offer some needed additional security, especially to a single mother. Further, I've never had a dog graffiti any walls. So, if I had my druthers, I think I'd ban teenage boys before I banned pets. (I remember when my sons were teenagers, we basically sacrificed one wall of their bedroom to graffiti in hopes that we wouldn't see it anywhere else.)

Also, accepting pets makes Delinco properties more popular with prospective tenants, and the tenants tend to stay longer when they have pets. Again, turnover is the landlord's worst enemy.

Monitoring Your Property

In most states and counties, a landlord has the legal right to enter the property, although twenty-four-hour notice is usually required. I rarely exercise this right, as I observe that it causes more resentment from the tenant than solving any property damage issue. Hopefully, if we have properly screened the tenant and the outside of the house is fairly well-maintained, we're safe to assume the inside of the house is in adequate condition.

I found that one of the best ways to remind tenants that I am in constant surveillance of the property is to leave notices. Ken, among other landlords, has followed me with similar notices. The concept here is very straightforward: constantly reminding the tenant that you, and possibly even the property manager, are on site and insisting on proper maintenance of your property.

First, when I notice a banned activity is ongoing, I will immediately knock on the door to raise my objection—politely and with respect always. Whether that works or not, I will leave a notice, which makes it more difficult to forget. Below is one such notice:

> Dear Delino tenant _____,
> Re: inoperable vehicles on premises
>
> Please note the city of Fontana does not allow inoperable vehicles on residential house lots; such vehicles will be towed at the vehicle owner's expense. Also, there will be a storage fee to retrieve the vehicle.
>
> You have 30 days to repair and/or remove the vehicle.
>
> I will check back in two weeks, and/or would welcome your phone call with any progress.
>
> Sincerely Daryl Deliman,
> Delinco owner _____
> Date _____

These Delinco notices are always printed on colored card stock, and I call that evening to make sure the tenants received the orange inoperable vehicle notice and then inquire about their intentions. Other landlords use three-day notices to force tenants to correct any activity contrary to their rental or lease contract. Both are effective. I find my notices are immediate and perhaps less effort.

I also have notices on many other topics, such as the yard being neglected, especially not being watered; reminders that the rent is due on the tenth with a late fee of $80 after the tenth; a specific utility bill not being paid by the tenant (in this situation, I ask for proof of payment); and more topics of contract enforcement.

My notices to the tenants are consistent with the same theme, always referencing a higher authority than just me the owner, usually the city, county, or state regulations. Notices are businesslike and impersonal, often with the mutual goal of maintaining and improving the property.

Why leave a signed notice rather than sending an email or text? I'm trying to give a directive, not start a dialogue. We have too many tenants, so I really don't want to have a dialogue with any of them. The signed, posted notice is the easiest, most direct way of giving this directive. After all, they are living in my house. On occasion, I do use email or text if I don't get the results requested in the notice.

The three-day notice is a way to legally alert tenants that they are in violation of their rental contract. It is emphatic, as it is attached to the front door or given to the tenant by hand. Most commonly, the three-day notice is issued when tenants are late with rent. Many property managers will issue a three-day notice on the eleventh of the month if the rent is not yet received. I'm a little more lenient, usually waiting toward the end of the month to issue three-day notices unless I have had a specific discussion with the tenant regarding late rent and when it would be paid.

However, the three-day notice can be used to notify the tenant that they are in violation of other lease contract requirements. In most states, a three-day notice initiates the eviction process.

CHAPTER 6

Handyman, or Do You Want to Take That Urgent Call?

In starting Delinco properties, my brother announced early that he didn't want to be the landlord who had to respond to a tenant's urgent call on weekends or evenings. Of course, no one needs that sort of urgency dropped on their doorstep. I didn't relish the idea, as I have limited blue-collar skills and live too far away.

To minimize your effort and travel, it is ideal to have a handyman who can respond quickly on most tenant demands. Best if he lives near the rental properties. We have enough houses to have a handyman sometimes full-time.

Abilities and levels of a handyman for your real estate properties include fixing or installing plumbing projects; light to medium carpenter carpentry, including walls, doors, etc.; and low-risk electrical projects. In California and most states, your handyman will need to be English and Spanish bilingual, and should also be pleasant and socially acceptable. It's an added bonus if he can visit the tenant to collect rents and possibly negotiate a repayment plan on payments when rents are past due.

Augusto has been that handyman for Delinco for many years, as he has most of these traits on most days. Javier, then Chris preceded him. He often has an assistant with him, a specific assistant for different types of work. Of course, these assistants have varied over the years.

This relationship is a two-way street. Sometimes, he'll call me and say he needs to make money, so what work is needed on my properties? We will agree on a house that needs painting, or I keep a list of other upgrades needed. Roofs are in constant need of patching or replacing. Perhaps a chore as small as planting two citrus trees at a house with a cooperating tenant will suffice until we get a more urgent call from a tenant. To support a full-time handyman, hence be certain my houses are his 1st priority, I have to assure he earns a minimum amount of money, about $4,500 each month.

Electrical work certainly is the most dangerous item on the list. Many people don't realize that an electrical impulse as low as one tenth of an Amp, 0.10 Amp, can kill a person. Certainly every house has much more power than that, as most houses are engineered at 100 to 200 Amps. A family friend, an electrician by trade, somehow was killed in his own home despite his expertise.

The instruction I give Augusto is to review the electric project requirements, then turn off the power to the house before actually doing the work. It's certainly inconvenient to the tenant, but safety first. Also, I instruct him to walk away if he's not 100 percent sure he can do the job safely. I hire outside electricians more than any other type of service.

Regarding the need to be pleasant and socially acceptable: we have many tenants who are single mothers, so they are very concerned about the people who enter their residence. Augusto and his team can be brusque and even abrasive, as they have a specific job to do and want to get it completed as quickly and with as little effort and dialogue as possible. I have had to lecture Augusto about being more cordial, dressing better, and even personal hygiene for him and his handyman team. For some single mothers, I have called to assure them that Augusto is trustworthy, married, and a father, but he just wants to finish quickly and leave.

Actually, there's a local plumber who advertises that his team are the smell-good plumbers. Women are more sensitive to smell and have more acute smelling sensors than men, so it's more significant that any strange man entering their domicile does not noticeably stink.

Regarding rent collection: Often, Augusto has become at least a trusted person for many of the tenants, so he does attempt to collect rents and negotiate repayment plans for those who are in arrears. This can become a problem if the tenant wants to continue paying Augusto and obtaining a receipt for the rent, as I'm then obligated to pay Augusto the going rate of 8 percent on any rent he collects.

My agreement with Augusto is that he will collect rents and get paid this 8 percent only if the tenant is over thirty days late and I specifically ask him to visit and negotiate with the tenant. Once the tenant is current with the rent, everything goes back to normal, and the tenant sends me the rent or deposits to my account, and Augusto is no longer paid 8 percent.

Of course, I do pay Augusto just to show up and attempt to collect the rent or negotiate a repayment plan. Legally, a third party can be useful, as an owner negates a three-day notice by contacting the delinquent tenant directly.

Almost all tenants have additional work they want us to do on their houses. There are many ways to handle this, much of it depending on the tenant's status. If they're good tenants who take good care of the house and makes payments on time, you certainly want to accommodate to keep them happy so they won't move. I try to honor most tenant requests if it truly is an upgrade to the house, as long as it's not too expensive and is truly an upgrade and not just a personal selection. Another favorite is, I will pay for the parts, the paint, the plants and fertilizer, or whatever, if the tenant supplies the labor on these mutually beneficial projects.

Augusto has been instructed to respond to all tenant emergencies quickly, and specifically without contacting me. Since he's been with Delinco for many years, I trust his judgment on the necessity or urgency of the work. He knows he has a limit of $1,000 before contacting me for permission with a full estimate.

This is my response to the noted downside of being a landlord: the tenant emergency. A working relationship with a handyman can usually save you this stress.

Jesus was a carpenter, and I would trust him not to pad hours. For all others, trust but verify. While I trust the handyman and most of the outside contractors I utilize, if they know the owner will not inspect and recognize the effort required, rest assured they won't resist the temptation to pad the invoice, especially hours required.

Finally, most of our business world operates and pays on net thirty days. To maintain best relations with handymen and contractors, I pay immediately, on the spot, by check or cellphone direct bank transfer. They need the money, and often forwarded their own money for supplies, so immediate payment in appreciated. In response, when called, they are ready to work for Delinco ASAP.

CHAPTER 7

Upgrading the Property

Always when selecting a property to acquire, you should be thinking of how you can upgrade the property to improve its livability, perhaps even expanding livable space. With the tendency toward affordable housing, many states and counties allow you to add an accessory dwelling unit (ADU) to existing property, sometimes without a permit. Our objective in upgrading is to increase the rent, and in general to make it a more livable unit.

Upgrades are not always necessary, as your property will probably increase in value with inflation and commensurate annual rent increases. Some casual landscaping can always make the property more attractive.

Pardon the blatant sexism, but too often I find that women (tenants, property manager, wife) involved in my real estate investments want upgrades of personal preference—perhaps painting a certain lighter color, or a bathroom or kitchen remodel. Meanwhile, we men are usually thinking of how much we can increase the rent when we complete this upgrade.

Considering buying a house that might be a little bit too small as a rental? I prefer 1,100 square feet or greater, three-bedroom, two-bath houses. Some older houses are smaller, and room additions are very expensive, if you can get a permit. What has worked for me on two previous occasions is adding a tough shed (commercial name Tuff Shed). A tough shed of twelve feet by ten feet does not need to be permitted in most counties, and is only $3,800 currently.

In one case, it was literally a godsend to one stepmother, as she was able to "relocate" her stepson and his drums to the shed mounted on a concrete slab in the backyard. We connected power underground. So stepson, his drums, and his band could practice and disturb no one. Maybe that's how Ritchie Valens got started.

Well, almost no one was disturbed, as their dog ran off.

A tough shed extra room has also been used as an office, playroom, or extra bedroom. Careful, though—some neighbors may protest the extra bedroom concept. But today, with the new accessory dwelling unit (ADU) acceptance laws (see chapter 14 on trends), their complaints would probably fall on deaf ears.

Adding a full ADU with two or three very small rooms—some are listed online for about $15,000—may not even require a permit in many California counties with the new laws pushing affordable housing. You would need to be selective to assure increased rent to cover your expanded unit. (See chapter 14 for more on ADUs.)

For upgrades, we are all looking to slap on a coat of paint, install a couple of plants, and increase the value by $15,000 to 20,000. Although that's sometimes possible, it usually takes a bit more effort.

In California and most Southwestern states, citrus trees grow well. Certainly, a mature, producing citrus tree, lemon or orange, adds to the value of a house. However, are you sure your tenant will water it? With a cooperative tenant, adding two to four citrus trees is beneficial. Too often, the tenant does not want to waste money (actually it's just a few cents per month) to water plants. So foliage adding color but requiring little water or other attention are ideal. I've added bougainvillea to most of my properties.

Everyone wants a fine trimmed, green-grass yard in front and possibly even in back of their home, correct? A nice, safe place for the kids to play. In many counties, you can be cited if your lawn is not maintained and is dying or has gone brown. However, more recently in California, where drought is the norm rather than the exception, the expression is "brown is the new green."

If my tenant requests a lawn and commits to maintaining it, we will add fertilizer and grass seed and work with him to have a lawn in front. More often these days, the yard is just neglected. Green grass in front certainly improves the appearance, hence the property value, but an owner can waste thousands of dollars if the tenant won't maintain.

Certainly, periodic painting is a necessity, but be sure to choose a popular, current color. You may want to consider re-stuccoing. At just twice the cost, re-stuccoing can give the house a new, more modern look.

One of our better tenants, at one of our better four-bedroom, two-bath houses, insisted she had to have a kitchen remodel. So Augusto and I visited her and reviewed what she wanted upgraded in what was legitimately a dirty, old, outdated kitchen. We took notes, listened, and said we would proceed.

Augusto was able to do most of the work, but he had to go to an outside contractor for part of the plumbing. The total cost was a whopping $4,900, with nine separate kitchen items purchased plus the installation thereof. Later, I discussed this upgrade with Jose, my major partner in apartment buildings. Jose told me he had upgraded three kitchens for what I had paid for one. Ouch! I hate to be informed that I've overspent unnecessarily.

So Jose took me to one of the apartments and showed me his kitchen upgrade. Also, he made sure the tenant was there so she could confirm that she was most appreciative of the kitchen upgrade. Apparently, Jose had gone online to obtain three prefab kitchens, with dual sink cabinets, eight feet of sink board, and more, for a shocking comparatively low $920. Jose installed it, took a more than one day, and estimated a handyman would charge about $700 for this prefab kitchen install.

Noted, upgrading kitchens and bathrooms can be a major expense, but you can obtain a prefab bathroom—just sink and cabinet and mirror—for about $350. The prefab kitchen will be more today than Jose and I paid previously, probably closer to $1,200 now. It's still a great deal less expensive than doing an item-by-item upgrade, and it looks very new and modern.

Comparison between single-family houses and multiunit buildings often comes down to cash flow and turnover. While I am still a partner on a couple of small apartment buildings, I leave the management to the major partners, as turnover requires more constant attention. On the plus side, when positive cash flow is higher, you commensurately increase the value of the building. A rough rule of thumb suggests there is a 100:1 ratio of monthly rent to value. So if you can increase the rent by $100/month, the value of the investment property increases by $10,000. Many other factors are involved, but the concept of raised rents = increased value is always true.

CHAPTER 8

Section 8 Housing Authority: Embrace or Avoid

For those of you who are not familiar with the Section 8 Housing Authority program, let me offer this statement presented by our government directly from the Internet:

> The housing choice voucher program is the federal governments major program for assisting very low income families the elderly and the disabled to afford decent safe and sanitary housing in the private market. Since housing assistance is provided on behalf of the family or individual participants are able to find their own housing, including single-family houses town houses and apartments. The participant is free to choose any housing that needs the requirements of the program and it's not limited to unit located in subsidize housing projects.

Housing choice vouchers are administered locally by the public housing agencies (PHAs). In some areas, mostly low-income apartment buildings, Section 8 may be the only game in town for full occupancy. In most other areas it is a viable option for landlords in any at mid- to lower-level income areas.

First, a parent of a family must get qualified through Section 8 based on income and family members. Next, the qualified tenant selects a house or apartment of interest. Assume the qualified tenant selects your house or apartment. Since there is government money involved, you know there are strings attached.

A Section 8 inspector must inspect your property to qualify. Often, there are requirements to upgrade to supposed standards, but often to the inspector's various peculiarities. I mention this as I've seen tremendous variety in what some inspectors will pass and others will require improvement. They have a checklist, so there is not supposed to be this sort of variability. Usually, the requirements are reasonable, and they are upgrades that are of mutual benefit and needed. But sometimes, it seems the upgrade is from left field and irrelevant.

On some occasions, there are structural requirements that might be quite expensive and difficult and that others would consider unnecessary. I disqualified one of my houses as a doorframe was too low and the inspector insisted it be replaced—$2,000 and an unnecessary project.

Many landlords will not accept Section 8 tenants; it's sometimes even stated in their listing. Most often this inspection, which is annual also, is the reason. While you can obtain a listing of Section 8 requirements, as mentioned, there's a great variability in how a particular inspector applies these requirements.

When working with Section 8, we have determined it is in our best interest to meet with the inspector and stay with him as he inspects the property. This is both for the initial inspection and the annual inspection. These are reasonable people, so I have reached compromises with them: "OK, Jim, how about I paint the interior before your tenant moves in this year, and next year we will replace the floor?" He responds, "That'll work, Daryl. Will count on a good paint job now and new flooring next year."

The good news is that Section 8 usually pays top dollar for the area and that dwelling designation. If the going rate for a three-bedroom two-bath house in your area is $2,000, chances are they will authorize a payment of $2,100 for a qualified tenant.

Note that Section 8 usually just pays the major portion of that authorized amount. The tenant might be responsible for 15 to 35 percent of the authorized payment. A contract or letter update from Section 8 to you and the tenant defines these amounts.

Often, tenants will try to buddy up to you and suggest they be allowed to pay less than the required amount, or they don't want to pay the required amount. Other landlords have accepted less. I always respond, "No, that is dangerous. You as tenant could lose Section 8 qualification, and this could disqualify me from any further Section 8 contracts." Further, I tell the tenant that Section 8 requires that I verify that tenants are paying their full portion of the rent (which occasionally happens, but uncommon). Finally, I say, "Let's do this one by the book."

When the family structure changes—i.e., someone moves out—things can get sticky. With a smaller family, Section 8 will pay less and/or suggest the tenant move. Often, the tenant won't want to move, or may try to force you to accept lower rent. Alternatively, they will lie to Section 8 about changes in family structure. If Section 8 is notified that the family structure has decreased by a member, then they also may force you to accept a lower rent.

Again, I have found Section 8 is somewhat negotiable on this point. In one such instance, the Section 8 agent required me to write a letter requesting higher rent. My note was simple: "The going rate for this area is $2,000 a month for a three-bedroom, two-bath house. I need $2,000 a month for this house, and I don't want to force this family to move." Section 8 agents and inspectors are reasonable people and have some negotiating latitude, so I got my rent for this house and did not have to force the tenant to move.

Ron, who owns apartment buildings in Orange County, comments that "Sometimes the wrong Section 8 tenant can ruin the culture of a building. May have gang affiliations or something. Regarding inspections, I have found their inspectors to be reasonable to negotiate with. One wanted me to replace a tile floor, as there were cracked tiles. I went to cheaper linoleum, and they had no issue. Passed inspection."

Jake owns units in Santa Monica, San Pedro, and sections of South Los Angeles. He informs us that Section 8 is not necessary and rarely considered in the more upscale Santa Monica area. However, in San

Pedro and in many sections of South LA lower-income areas, Section 8 may be the only game in town to fill your units.

Further, Jake presents the Section 8 website and reminds us that Section 8 also administers for the Veterans Administration. The process of working with Section 8 is initiated often by going to their website and listing your units for rent with full description. From there, a Section 8– or Veterans Administration–approved tenant contacts you and asks to see the unit. After reviewing their information, the landlord is totally in control. You are not obligated to show the unit or consider this tenant.

Sometimes, Section 8 offers bonuses of up to $2,500 to place their tenant in your unit immediately, as part of their goal is to get poor people off the street and into adequate housing. Jake tells us that Section 8 tenants tend to stay longer. As expected, there is a broad variety of Section 8 tenants. Some are just trying to use the system and will not respect your property, but most want to maintain their voucher, so they will maintain the property and play by the landlord's rules.

Jake further suggests that you inspect the property routinely so you can report and possibly even issue a three-day notice if there are unwanted activities. So, using Section 8, the landlord has clout, even in evictions. Often, when an eviction is threatened, tenants will be very concerned about losing their Section 8 voucher and will move out sooner than the usual four to six months required for a standard eviction.

Also, the Section 8 manager will forward your calls with the tenant and force quicker eviction. The security deposit with Section 8 is twice the monthly rent, which is usually but not always adequate to cover any damage. Again, these are lower-income folks who quite often won't respect your property.

Also, Jake seems to have more problems with addicts, but again, you can usually quickly evict an addict from your property. Currently, the worst type of addicts are methamphetamine users. But again, you can usually quickly evict them from your property.

CHAPTER 9

Expanding Your Real Estate Portfolio and Phases

Once you've gotten started with a rental property, what is the safest, easiest way to expand your real estate portfolio? Are the economic times encouraging for expanding your real estate portfolio? I recommend that you check the important parameters, such as loan interest rate, unemployment rate, vacancy rate, and new building permits in your area of interest. Also, do you have access to additional capital in case of an unexpected downturn? Assuming all parameters are positive, let's forge ahead patiently but not get financially overextended.

Financing Options

Conservative, Low-Risk Plan

One of the lowest-risk, most conservative real estate investing plans was completed by a childhood neighbor of mine. Dean and I used to build forts out of wood, secured by locks and hinges, but not just an average wooden fort an eleven-year-old would build. These had doors that fit without air gap and flooring fully covering with tight corners, as one of us was already an excellent craftsman.

At our Narbonne High School twenty-year reunion, Dean told me his plan for investing. Actually, Dean claimed it was not really a plan;

he just did what he enjoyed, upgrading houses. He and his wife both worked in the aerospace and defense industry and made good money—high five figures. They lived in Torrance, so they would buy a house owner-occupied, only 10 percent down and best loan, since they'd both achieved excellent FICO scores. Then they'd live there a year or two while Dean would upgrade, often high-quality upgrades that would justify higher rents, as Torrance is mixed but overall upscale. Then, they would buy another house nearby—owner-occupied, so only 10 percent down required.

Most of us, when we change residences, sell one house to buy the next using the accrued equity. Instead, Dean and his wife would save their excess income from their nine-to-five jobs, turn the original home into a rental, and buy a new fixer-upper. Maybe not a real fixer-upper, but an older home in an area that would appreciate upgrades and modernization. They repeated this process five times, yielding five rentals plus their residence.

Torrance in those years was an area of improving real estate values. They increased about 10 to 15 percent per year, which was fortunate for Dean and his wife's plan. Obviously, it took almost ten years, but as I said in the introduction, patience is required. The end result for Dean and his wife was well over $1 million in equity with very positive cash flow. I congratulated my old neighbor on becoming a millionaire, and he sheepishly accepted.

Dean and I agreed, and he confirmed, that he did annually raise the rents as much as was reasonable, and we high-fived on jacking the rents up. Too many landlords become friends with their tenants and/or just forget to raise rents. Just a COLA increase is often enough, but sometimes the market will bear more.

Refinance One, Buy Another

For an aggressive real estate investment plan, when a property reaches 50 percent equity, maybe it's time to refinance, take the proceeds from the equity gain, and buy another investment property. The term my dad (Daniel Deliman, LA city teacher) used was *top-heavy*. For example, we bought the Sycamore Street house as part of the HUD 12, resulting in a loan on this property of $60,000. After owning it for just two years and upgrading, we now had a house worth about $140,000

So I applied for a loan to refinance the house at 80 percent of its current value. Lender agreed, so we refinanced at only a slightly higher rate of $100,000. Yields $40,000 as down payment for buying another investment house. More income tax depreciation to shelter my income from working as a regional manager for a scientific equipment company. (Note that I am rounding off and leaving out the commensurate fees for financing.)

The end result was two investment houses with productive debt (mortgage low enough to have positive cash flow assessed by PITIMM). There was potential for twice the equity gain with expected appreciation and improvements. The same tactic was used at least five times in the expansion of Delinco Properties.

Usually as real estate investors, we go through stages. As you probably noted with the team plan and with the start of Delinco, moving from residence to residence within your investment area is required. Sometimes family or job requirements will not allow moving residences. Most of us are entrenched in our current residence, so the "Dean plan" or other plans of changing residence are impractical.

More likely, you may want to put up to 20 percent, pay a slightly higher interest rate, and buy income property in the more traditional aforementioned route—to refinance one property, take the equity out, and buy another investment property. For those investing in multi units or small apartment buildings, the typical strategy is to sell the smaller apartment building, use the equity and your established financial track record and credibility with lenders, then buy a larger apartment building.

Of course, this goes with the usual plan of buying in an area of real estate appreciation, upgrading the building, increasing rents, etc. Again, real estate agents active in investment property tell me an increase of $1 is 100 x in establishing the value of the property. So if you can raise the rents on all the combined properties by $3,000, you've increased the property value by $300,000. This might take a few years obviously.

Attempting to raise rents too quickly can backfire, at any level, if it causes turnover.

I'm told many big-league real estate investors, including owners of sports teams, acquire their millions by the strategy of trading up in apartment buildings until they reached multiple apartment buildings, or one very large $10 million plus. They usually start with much more capital than available to most of us.

Note that refinancing an existing house is irrelevant to depreciation for tax shelter purpose (see chapter 11) and does not renew. You need to acquire new property to start the 27.5 years of depreciation.

Save or Borrow As Needed to Obtain the 20 Percent Down Payment

The most common plan seems to be raising enough capital for the 20 percent down payment to acquire income property. (This, of course, depends on your excess income.) When possible, this might be the best plan for most, as you don't pay the refinancing fees required in the previous plan of refinancing one property to buy two. Also, as loans get older, you amortize a higher percentage of the principal, thus gaining equity.

Use the 1031 Exchange: Sell One, Buy Two, and Defer Tax

So typically, you could sell the house for $400,000 and buy a triplex, or two houses for $700,000 while deferring taxes. More on this useful IRS tool in chapter 11 with our CPA.

Four Phases of Real Estate Investing

Allow me to offer four phases of real estate investing, assuming you don't have family money or any other source of major capital funds.

Phase 1

You and possibly a spouse are working professionals making better than average wages. You have reviewed possible investment options and have committed to real estate investing for all its possible advantages. You have maintained or are working to improve your FICO score. You are not yet in a family way and your profession allows you some latitude to work remotely, so you can consider taking advantage of the better owner-occupied financing, allowing you to move residences while initiating your real estate investment plan.

You have self-educated by reading such classics as *Creating Wealth* by Robert G. Allen and other real estate investing sources. As well as acquiring wealth, Mr. Allen advises on how not to waste it, as is too often an American habit (credit cards at up to 20 percent interest!).

Phase 2

You have acquired some income property, invested prudently, and have positive cash flow. Seeing some advantages in using the real estate property as a tax shelter, you are looking to expand your real estate portfolio but are no longer in a position to move residences. Perhaps you are looking to use equity you have acquired to refinance and buy more property—or, alternatively, have savings and excess income to acquire the capital to buy more investment property.

Phase 3

You have acquired enough property that you can qualify as a real estate professional and receive the full tax-shelter benefits (see chapter 10 re: tax shelters). Perhaps for a married couple, one of the two spouses qualifies as a real estate professional. You are still looking to acquire more property, but only within your guidelines of an ideal investment property. Very positive cash flow contributes significantly to your income, but you are still working professionally in other fields.

Phase 4 *(my current status)*

You have acquired enough property, with positive cash flow due to upgrading, inflation, and some loans being paid off. Therefore, you can retire from, or greatly reduce your hours in, your chosen profession. The depreciation tax advantage has expired on some or most of your houses, so to renew the depreciation advantage, you must sell one of the properties with expired depreciation and buy two more.

Enjoy the fruits of your labor and play. Travel our beautiful country or the world, Buy that overpriced sports car or boat. Assist family members financially, pay tuition for an aspiring family member, or whatever tickles your fancy.

Should you have another source of major capital funds, jump in at phase 2 or 3. Perhaps you have family money, or you are a professional athlete or entertainer. Note that professional athletes' careers are usually much shorter than anticipated. And the Screen Actors Guild has an unemployment rate of over 90 percent.

What??!! It takes 27.5 years to achieve phase 4? OK, while it took me that many years, dear reader, I offer my input so you can achieve your goals much more quickly (see especially chapter 12 on partners).

CHAPTER 10

Tax Benefits

Including an Interview with Don Saltikov, CPA

Claiming depreciation on investment properties is a fairly simple concept, but it becomes more complex when applied. It starts in this manner: Let's say you have an investment house worth $400,000. You then claim the land is worth $100,000, as land is not depreciable. And the building is worth $300,000. The building depreciates over the next 27.5 years. (I don't understand why this isn't a round number, but you know how Congress needs to compromise to get bills passed.)

So, over the next 27.5 years, you depreciate this building. Helps if you can legitimately claim and defend that you are a real estate professional. I think I became fully tax exempt with twelve houses while pulling a six-figure income.

Further tax advantages include the acquisition and depreciation of certain items that may be of common use in your day-to-day life but are also used in real estate. For example, currently I lease a car, and the main purpose is to drive to my properties. But of course, I use it for other purposes. Same for other materials, such as computers, tools, and anything else that might be of mutual usage. However, you can only claim and depreciate for the actual hours or percentage used in real estate. For example, I must report miles on the car used in real estate vs. personal miles. Finally, assuming you have an office in your home, that can be a tax write-off but is rather complex, so I have never attempted this tax advantage.

A key point of depreciation is rather obvious. As you have more real estate, you can shelter more of your income. Thus pay less income tax and have more money for a down payment on another investment property, or to upgrade existing properties.

Real Estate Professional, a simple overview

if you qualify as a real estate professional for a particular year you are not subject to the passive loss rules, thus the entire loss from real estate trades or businesses is deductible. To qualify as a real estate professional for a particular tax year, more than half your personal service performed during that year are in real estate trades or businesses and you spend more than 750 hours of service in real property trades or business in which you materially participate.

The above the above does not apply to licensed real state people and is meant to be a simple overview of the tax rules and regulation of rental property and you should seek the advice of a qualified tax advisor.

For an individual (non-real estate professional) who actively participates in rental activity.

Rental property is generally subject to the passive activity loss rules. Depreciation is only a part of the net loss or profit of a rental property. If a profit it is tax as ordinary income. If a loss it comes under the passive activity loss rules. The ability to take the loss depends on your taxable income as specially computed. An individual who actively participates in the rental activity may offset up to $25,000 ($12,500 if married filing separate) of nonpassive income with the portion of the passive activity loss from the rental property. If the loss is greater than $25,000 ($12,500 if married filing separate) the amount over $25,000/$12,500 is carried over until such time it can be use, see below, or the property is sold.

The $25,000/$12,500 loss is deductible if specifically computed income is not more than $100,000 and is reduced by 50% of income that exceeds $100,000 and phased out completely with income of $150,000.

Residential rental property is depreciated over 27 ½ years and commercial property over 39 years.

Active participation means participating in a significant and bona fide manner. Specifically computed income is income calculated without the real estate loss. Material participation can be one of seven participation tests, see your tax advisor.

My CPA was somewhat reluctant to allow me to claim that I was a real estate professional while I was still pulling six-figure salary selling lab equipment. We discussed the details, and I did confirm for him that I met all the criteria. Actually, I had cut back hours somewhat in the lab-equipment area while increasing my hours in landlording and scavenging for new properties. Not a claim you want to make recklessly and without meeting all the criteria. I'm sure an IRS auditor would scrutinize such a claim and require proof.

In fact, as a real estate broker or agent, in most states, you must state in the "offer to purchase" whether the offer is significantly under market—an effort to alleviate real estate agents or brokers taking advantage of naïve sellers. I've never been a real estate agent or broker, so I never had this restriction. My late brother Dennis was a broker, so all Delinco "lowball" offers were in my name.

IRS Audit

As real estate investors or even just taxpayers, we all want to avoid an IRS audit. In best case, it will require probably forty hours of accounting, finding receipts, and perhaps a $3,000 fee to your CPA. In worst case, that plus additional taxes and penalties will be owed. After a successful audit by the IRS, with additional taxes and penalties assessed, you are now on the IRS radar for future audits.

Soon after I had bought out my partners, I received an audit notice from the IRS. I was certainly concerned, but since I was well advised early, I was prepared with files of receipts, rental contracts, bank statements, and other commensurate documents. So you can understand that one of my first questions to the IRS auditor was why was I selected for this audit. My CPA interrupted me, telling me later that he did not want to initiate the IRS audit with conflict.

Anyway, between my CPA and me, we had all the receipts and documentation to justify all the deductions. Three hours later, our IRS auditor was so impressed with our honesty and full documentation that she actually told me about a small deduction that I had missed. Anyway, I had to ask the same question again, as I would like to know, and I think I had the right to know, why I was selected for an IRS audit ? This time, she did answer, just saying that the computer popped my name out, as some of the ratios were incongruous.

In further discussions with Don Saltikov, a very seasoned CPA, he confirmed that in the computer processing of a tax return, certain ratios of entries are expected, and numbers outside the range will trigger attention. Basically, any deduction that seems too large could garner you the attention you want to avoid. Also, Don says, egregious errors of any sort may trigger the computer to require an accountant to review your return. Also, Don says, it can just be dumb luck—kind of like the lottery and your number came up.

I have, and maybe you have also, been contacted regarding a discrepancy in my tax return. My lender stated a value of $1,400 for the mortgage tax deduction on one of my loans, which had to be extremely low, as the monthly payment was $650 per month and the loan was in the twelfth year of a twenty-five-year term. So I entered the correct amount and had an inquiry from the IRS. I quickly justified my correct amount and heard nothing further from the IRS, as they accepted my explanation.

Currently, we all recognize that IRS auditors are overworked. Rumor has it that this administration wants to hire over 80,000 additional IRS auditors. That's a rather scary consideration for us real estate investors, and we must question the competence of that many auditors hired so quickly.

Expanding Using the 1031 Exchange

In expanding your real estate portfolio, the 1031 Exchange is a valuable tool to defer paying capital gains tax. It refers to section 1031 of the IRS code. It is complex, and it does affect depreciation, recapture, and more, so I suggest you consult with your CPA before attempting to use the 1031 Exchange tool.

For our purposes, I will offer the following example: You want to expand your real estate portfolio, so you sell your investment house worth $400,000. You don't accept the proceeds from this sale but instead transfer it to a qualified intermediary as required by the 1031 Exchange process. From there, you have forty-five days to identify the like-kind property you want to acquire and 180 days to close the transaction.

The like-kind rule is really quite broad, as you can buy land, an apartment building, and several houses, but not artwork or stocks or anything out of the realm of real estate investment property. The 200 percent rule allows you to identify unlimited replacement properties as long as their cumulative value does not exceed 200 percent of the value of the property you have sold. So typically, you could sell the house for $400,000 and buy a triplex for $700,000, thus deferring the capital gain while expanding your real estate portfolio.

Don offers this warning with his statements in this chapter on tax advantages: Comments stated here are current to this year. As prudent real estate investors, it is imperative that we consult with a CPA and/or study the always-changing tax laws. Thanks, Don.

Being Tax-Exempt

My colleagues in scientific instrumentation queried me often about my real estate investments, especially after they heard that I was tax-exempt. They weren't supposed to hear this, but somehow the CFO or another manager released that personal item of my finances. It is controversial. Few people are tax-exempt, and that invites conjecture.

I always answered honestly but preferred to limit the information I released.

Based on their questions, it was obvious my colleagues were fraught with misconceptions about real estate investing. Most were highly educated but with limited access to accurate information, and they had heard many rumors—both success stories and horror stories. As noted in the introduction, my intent here is to present all aspects of real estate investing.

Almost all of us in scientific instrumentation are well educated and earn incomes in the low six figures. So the concept of tax exemption is certainly desirable, especially for us in the heavy tax-burden state of California. Human nature being what it is, certainly there was resentment of anyone who apparently isn't paying their 35 percent or more in income tax. To stave off the resentment, I would explain, or present, that I had paid at least $40,000 annually in property taxes on my various rental properties. So Uncle Sam gets his due one way or another.

Being overly cautious and conservative, most of my colleagues in scientific instrumentation still suffer in a higher tax bracket. More than a few offered to partner with me in my next real estate venture, but I can only see a downside for me in such a partnership.

CHAPTER 11

Anecdotes

In my 30+ years of landlording, there have been many peculiar and unforeseen occurrences. Many offer an obvious moral, some suggest better money management, and some are just amusing. Following are a few of the most memorable.

SWAT Team on Your Property

So a nosy neighbor calls me and says, "Daryl, why is the SWAT team surrounding your house here on Golden?"

My response: "I have no idea, but I guess I better drive over and find out. Please call me back again if you learn anything."

I arrived at my rental house after the incident was apparently completed. The SWAT team with their usual battering ram had demolished the front door (it was unlocked, but that's no fun). I went inside, where neighbors and family members were surrounding my tearful tenant and her stunned daughter. They were inside the family room, past another demolished door (this door had no lock).

As the story unfolded, an eight-year-old playmate was riding her bicycle looking for the daughter living at this rental house of mine. She rode up the driveway and noticed a man in an army uniform waving a pistol at the mother and daughter. She wisely went home and told her mother, who called 911. The 911 operator and the police were reluctant to believe an eight-year-old child, so they sent a police officer to surveil the property. He went to a neighbor's house for a better vantage point of this family room, confirmed what the eight-year-old child had seen, and immediately called for the SWAT team.

Apparently, the dad had been recently discharged dishonorably from the army for drug use. He had no visitation rights for the same reason. Through mutual friends, he managed to find where his ex-wife had moved with their daughter and intruded to visit. The incident ended peacefully enough, as only a suicidal fool would attempt to use a pistol to challenge the firepower of the SWAT team. He was cowering in the closet and wisely threw his pistol out and surrendered as instructed by SWAT.

Supposedly there is funding for repairing buildings after the SWAT team has "visited," but my letters to the San Bernardino sheriff went unanswered. (I was restricted from pursuing further by common sense, as the sheriff's crime lab was a customer in my lab equipment sales role; I had sold them Micro Fourier Transform Infrared Spectroscopy for trace evidence identification). In the end, I only had to replace two old doors and was pleased the incident ended without further violence. The front door was unlocked , but hey that's no fun. Bedroom door had no lock.

My tenant and her daughter moved out the next day and left no orwarding address. I assume the dad was charged, but I made no attempt to follow the story.

Moral: Ask more questions about your tenant's family situation.

Who Should Pay the Trash Bill?

When I presented Mr. Deadbeat Tenant with his overdue trash bill, he told me he could barely afford the rent and that the trash should be paid by the owner anyway. We disagreed, so I showed him on the contract where it says tenant is responsible for all utilities, including trash disposal.

Some weeks later, I arranged the "cash for keys" exchange with Mr.

Deadbeat Tenant, and he vacated the property after signing my brief letter. I conducted a brief search and saw nothing out of the ordinary.

A new tenant family moved into the property the next month, and everything was going well. Augusto had cleaned the house up; some painting was required, but there was no major damage. I raised the rent, of course.

Then the new tenant called me and asked: "Daryl, why is my dog always sniffing and digging in one area of the backyard?"

Next day, I walked back there with Augusto, and something kind of stunk. We looked around, we followed the dog, and his nose confirmed it. Augusto got his shovel and started digging. No, not a corpse, just many, many bags of trash. The deadbeat tenant had dug and dropped in shallow holes, just deep enough to cover the trash bags, and threw just enough dirt over so it wasn't evident. He had even buried an old TV.

In retrospect, I would've been bucks ahead to pay the trash bill sooner, which I was stuck with anyway as the owner of the property. We removed all the trash. Augusto made a run to the dump, then got some fill dirt to smooth out the backyard and apologized to the new tenant.

Moral: Pay their trash bill now, when deadbeat tenants demand it, or find out later, the hard way, where they hid their trash.

Property Manager from Hell

While I emphasize stability, I have had rotating property managers over the years. One will always stay in my mind. Hellen seemed friendly enough and had been in the business for seven years. However, I was a minor client to her, with only a couple of houses available to list with her for rent. She had other major clients, so she would place the best tenants with her major clients and leave me with the second-rate tenants.

At least one of the second-rate tenants was placed in one of my best houses, a nice four-bedroom unit in Highland. That new tenant was current with the rent for only the first three months and then started getting further behind. I was with Hellen once when she was called him, and I was appalled at her dialogue with him. She told him told him we were going to put him and his family out in the street and got very personal, saying, "What kind of bum are you, you can't put a roof over your family's heads." She used his children's names, saying, "Julie, Joe, and Bobby, you're going to be put in the street soon."

Later that week, the tenant called me, referring to Hellen as a bitch and saying how he was disgusted with her. He was going through tough times and would be able to go on a payment plan with us. I tried to intercede in this souring relationship, but Hellen insisted she was in charge and she would get us paid.

The tenant got further behind in rent. Hellen said, "Don't worry about it" and "He'll pay up soon, or through the money judgment in eviction."

Obviously, the tenant was very angry. He had no further conversations with me, but he did move his family out. Then he and a friend vandalized the house. After repairing obvious vandalism and other usual maintenance, repainting, and totaling all losses including lost rent, it was about $23,000 to rehab this house before we got another tenant placed—the most ever in my thirty-plus years as a property owner.

Obviously, I terminated our relationship with Hellen and her property management company and went to Propman. This time, I made sure that our house was listed on their board and through the Internet and the tenants could select the house they wanted. Therefore, my house would have an equal chance of getting a quality tenant.

Hellen did go to court against my original tenant and was able to get a money judgment, but certainly not for all the vandalism. Five years later, this angry tenant has not paid a dime on the money judgment. Hellen was dead wrong on this issue, as usual.

Moral: You are the owner, intercede when necessary.

Meth Lab?

I got a call from San Bernardino County Sheriff's Deputy Johnson, saying, "Mr. Deliman, are you the owner of the house at XXXX Lawson Rd., Highland?"

"Yes, I am."

"We suspect there is a methamphetamine lab in operation in the garage of that house. We think your tenant Joe Blow is operating a meth lab and selling in the area."

"Well, apparently, Deputy Johnson, he's not very good at it, as he's behind in the rent."

Deputy Johnson was not amused by my attempt at humor. (A fatal stab at humor, as my mother, Marvel Deliman, the playwright, would comment).

"Mr. Deliman, are you aware that you could be criminally liable if there is a meth lab on your property?"

"Deputy Johnson, I'm a law-and-order type of landlord. I donated to the San Bernardino County Sheriff's recent charity drive, sold equipment to your Crime lab. and I will proceed with eviction immediately."

While I don't think he was correct in any criminal liability on my part, as he didn't cite a statute, but I didn't want to find out the hard way.

I continued, "Deputy Johnson, I had a problem some years ago with your SWAT team coming into my property on Golden, as there was significant damage to the property and I was not compensated. How about this: I'll visit the property tomorrow, and we will try to get him out immediately. Next, I will provide you with a forwarding address for Joe Blow and his accomplices."

"Thank you, Mr. Deliman. I will expect a phone call from you on Monday."

So I called Joe Blow and left a very specific message. I visited the next day, saw him in person, and gave him the alert. I told him he had to move out immediately, as the sheriff was getting a search warrant.

One of the many bad traits of a meth head is paranoia, so he was very scared and in agreement that he should move out immediately. He said he would take no longer than two days. Not good enough, I retorted, as I assured him Monday the sheriff would be back with the search warrant and handcuffs. I instructed him to move out today, Saturday, and Sunday. I sent Augusto to help move him on Saturday.

I followed through, called Deputy Johnson on Monday, and told him the house was vacated, and he was correct: there was a meth lab in operation in the garage. I did offer the forwarding address, and Deputy Johnson was very pleased and thanked me for my support of law and order. Actually, it was a win-win situation, as eviction was forthcoming anyway, and it was the fastest eviction I've ever done. Further, I didn't have to offer any cash for keys.

Moral: Support your local police. They are us.

Your Pet Is a ?

This one is from my late brother's widow, Kay, also a real estate agent. Many years ago, Dennis had his eye on a house nearby in the high desert, we think Apple Valley. It was listed for sale by owner (common term is the acronym FoSBO). Dennis was convinced that we could turn it into an excellent rental, and we could obtain the property at a bargain price. Only a little upgrade was needed. The house was of adequate size, and there was also a shed in the back, where the owner kept a donkey.

Dennis knocked on the door, met with the woman, and expressed his interest, later concluding she could expect an offer very soon. After showing him the full property, she said thanks and that she would look forward to hearing from him.

Dennis returned after discussing financing, and met with the woman a second time, as he was prepared to make an offer. All she wanted to talk about was the damn donkey. It was apparent that she wasn't ready to consider his offer just yet. She didn't say no, but she did procrastinate.

A week later, Dennis was crestfallen, as that house had been taken off the market; the FoSBO sign was removed. He did knock on the door and talk with the woman again. She offered her regrets to Dennis, as she had sold her house to another man. This other gentleman had promised that he would keep the donkey and take care of it.

Moral: The hot button for sellers is usually price, but not always. Ask!

Handyman Did What?

The Delinco accountant would usually call a tenant when it was past the tenth and the rent had not been received. This particular tenant was habitually late, so she anticipated our call and was proactive. As soon as she answered the phone call from our naïve accountant, she immediately got aggressive, asking, "Why did your handyman, Augusto, take a shower in my house?"

The accountant was flustered and had not been expecting to have to field such a question. She listened to the tenant, and they had a further discussion about Augusto's alleged activity. The accountant was patient and seem to commiserate with this single mother.

I heard the story and immediately scoffed. As promised, I did call Augusto to clarify and just let him know what this tenant was saying. He was disgusted by such a baseless accusation and repeated what I had already told the accountant: he only lives thirty minutes away, and he would never shower at a tenant's house. But he did turn the shower on for about thirty seconds to rinse off his hands and his tools, as he had just completed some work on the bathroom sink. He referred me to his invoice, which verified this sink work.

I then called the tenant. Since we had met several times, she knew better than to try to bamboozle me, and so she promised to send the rent and a late fee when she got paid that Friday. While I didn't specifically call this tenant a liar, in my conversation I just did not give her the opportunity to tell her story. There was no further discussion of Augusto's supposed shower at the tenant's house.

Moral: There is no bigger or more creative liar than a tenant behind on rent.

"The Police Shot My Dog in the Ass!"

As mentioned, I prefer to buy houses in what would be considered a blue-collar area, as is most of the Inland Empire. However, when we bought the twelve houses bulk, several of the houses were in somewhat rougher areas. So when Sherry, a single mother, wanted to move in to the house on Macy, I was pleased but concerned. She immediately asked permission to have a dog to help protect her and her family—a very reasonable request from a single mother in this rougher neighborhood of the IE.

We discussed what kind of dog she would get, and she was emphatic that it would be a guard dog to keep her and her family safe, not your common household pet. So we reviewed with Augusto, our handyman, to assure that he could do his work without threat from this guard dog. No problem, Sherry assured us; whenever Augusto was coming over, the guard dog would be chained—just don't make any surprise, unannounced visits. Seemed like a working plan.

What was not part of the plan was a surprise visit by a truancy officer. Apparently, her son had more fun visiting a friend playing video games than going to elementary school. Truancy officers usually want to surprise the culprit and the parents rather than make an announced visit.

"The police shot my dog in the ass!" Sherry screamed at me over the phone.

The whole story unraveled. The truancy officer didn't see any indication of a dog, so he opened the gate and was walking to the front door when the dog barked and attacked the truancy officer. He pulled his service gun and shot once, wounding but not killing the dog and certainly scaring him off. (Further evidence of this rough neighborhood—a truancy officer carrying a service gun?) The officer then continued his visit.

Sherry complained further, "What do I do now?" Apparently, the dog was wounded but would survive and could still serve as a gimpy guard dog.

I reluctantly paid the vet bill, recognizing circumstances could've been much worse for all parties involved. Of course, I insisted she get proper signs warning of the dog. I'm sure her son regularly attends school, as he doesn't want another such visit.

Moral: Warning signs are needed if you have a guard dog.

Trained cockroaches?

It has always struck me as curious that some tenants so often want to complain about the handymen. Seems they would appreciate having them visit their home to correct a problem or upgrade. However, some tenants just need a reason to complain or blame.

So Mrs. Weinberger at Plum Avenue complained that Augusto and his team had brought cockroaches outside her house when they were painting for three days. No cockroach problem inside, as she kept a clean house. So she asked us to spray for cockroaches immediately. Of course, any exterminator worth his spraygun wouldn't spray only the exterior for cockroaches, they would need to spray interior and exterior. She still insisted there were no cockroaches inside that the cockroaches have been brought by Augusto and his team and cockroaches were outside. My property manager and I had a good chuckle at the suggestion of these exterior-trained cockroaches, brought in the handymen's lunchbags - knowing of course that the cockroach problem was fully Mrs. Weinberger's. Augusto, on the other hand was offended and disgusted by the baseless accusation and any cockroach suggestion, despite the fact we dismissed her accusation

. Anyway, we did spray the house inside and out for cockroaches. However, I did explain to Mrs. Weinberger that when she moved in the house it was freshly painted and certainly free of any cockroaches or any other pests, so it was mutually evident that we weren't fooled by her complaint.

Moral: while you may have to listen to your tenants, you don't have to take all their complaints seriously

CHAPTER 12

Partners, Including Spouses

Benny, a longtime family friend, comments, "Daryl, pleased to see you've finally achieved your goal in real estate investing. I'm sure you would've gotten there much sooner if it weren't for the divorce, and had you not had to buy out your family partners." I think Benny got his degree in sarcasm from the department of redundancy department at WhatsamatterU. However, part of my reason for writing this book, dear reader, is that perhaps I can assist others to achieve their real estate investing goal in many years less than it took me.

Certainly, if you are married or in a committed relationship, shared goals for real estate investing are required for success. With shared goals, your real estate investing plans could even survive an amicable divorce. Our divorce regrettably wasn't amicable, and paying two divorce attorneys while splitting assets was a major setback.

Delinco Properties started as a family partnership, with apparent mutual goals which later became divergent goals. My plan has always been to hold properties long-term, perhaps refinance, and use the proceeds from the gained equity to buy additional properties. At first, it seemed these goals were mutual, but financial pressures may have resulted in more a immediate need for cash. Others then saw a benefit in making a quick buck flipping houses.

So after about three years of turmoil in a five-year partnership, I bought out my family partners. In retrospect, I doubt I could have bought the twelve HUD houses from that other investor without my late brother Dennis's credentials as a real estate broker and juris doctorate. Hence, Delinco Properties was off to a strong start before the turmoil began.

Back to Benny: Part of his issue was jealousy, as he had gotten started in the Inland Empire with some investment properties, then his wife pulled the plug. Divergent goals—he was a bit of a dreamer with big visions of easy success and claimed she had no future vision; she could only see the immediate impact on their family. Anyway, their family decision to withdraw and liquidate two duplexes and a house was perhaps for the best.

The intros to a few real estate investing books claim "Anyone can invest in real estate" or "I can make money in any real estate market" or the famous "Nothing down." In my thirty-year-plus tenure, I've seen many success stories, plus too many families or couples financially overextended, panic sales at a loss, and people stuck with loser properties. Credit ratings are negatively impacted. If they will sell to you with nothing down, why are they so desperate to unload this property? While I don't doubt there may be good intentions and at least a shred of truth to those claims, I propose we play the odds and buy—in an inclining market, with favorable economic tailwinds—our defined ideal rental income property.

If we had to do the Delinco partnership as a start-over, we would have written out our goals. Hopefully, they would have been mutual goals; if not, at least there would be an understanding of where our goals might diverge. In any partnership, an exit strategy is imperative, even if it may reduce enthusiasm. If we reach an impasse, a disagreement, a severe downturn, what is needed is a strategy for buyout with fair compensation for all parties. That could have limited my losses and the damaged family relations.

I had another partnership on a house in Fontana. We started with the "Dean plan," as my partner was an excellent craftsman and was going to upgrade a newer but vandalized house. Despite the poor condition, I got good financing with Jesse as an owner-occupant. The partnership went well. Jesse improved the house to the point we could leave it as an excellent rental, getting top dollar for the area after about ten months. However, he had a family medical emergency and needed tens of thousands of dollars immediately. We had a written exit strategy, so I bought him out, and we parted friends with plans for future real estate acquisitions. It was a win-win plan, and I still have that house as a profitable rental. Jesse says he will be ready again soon.

I am also a minor partner in a couple of small apartment buildings in the IE. All is going well, and I leave management to the major partners, mainly Jose. I receive an annual statement verifying our gains both in appreciation of the building value as well as positive cash flow as assessed by PITIMM. Certainly, I visit the buildings often, talk with tenants, inspect work, compare rents, check property title, etc. Again, an exit strategy is defined in writing, so I anticipate continued profits, selling the building, or buyout in the future.

While I'm focused on making all my own decisions in my real estate investments, certainly there are reasons to initiate a partnership. There is more financial clout and capital with two or more equal partners, allowing acquisition of larger or more property. Blending of roles or skills is something I have done well with—me offering the financing to acquire a property while my partner has the craft skill to improve it. Another successful partnership was buying a small apartment building where my partner resided and managed. In all cases, I recommend roles, and an exit strategy, be defined in writing.

CHAPTER 13

Minimizing Losses When Facing the Inevitable Downturn

Overextended Financially

Buoyed by endorsements from my MBA peers, I proceeded to buy more property in the Inland Empire—mostly houses. Like most beginning real estate investors, I became overextended before too long. You're really not sure when you're overextended until the first downturn occurs.

I've always resented and fought the lenders' approach to assessing rental income, as they apply a multiplier of 0.7 to your rental income. For example, if you have three houses with total rents of $6,000/month and PITIMM of $4,500/month, the lender will indicate you have negative monthly cash flow ($6,000 ' 0.7 = $4,200, less than PITIMM so negative cashflow). With my experience and the best practices noted previously, I usually have 100 percent occupancy. My highest vacancy rate ever is perhaps 12 percent. Hindsight suggests I should have applied their multiplier to my rental income before buying more properties.

When Southern California was hit with a recession in the early nineties, many of my tenants moved out, opting for cheaper rents with apartments. Others responded to a pink slip by moving back in with their parents. I actually lowered some rents to keep tenants staying and paying. In retrospect, I wish I'd had more Section 8 tenants then (I had only three). Then I could have survived this recession.

My predicament was that I had used all my capital funds to acquire more property. Delinco had quickly gone up to twenty-three houses with very little in funds in reserve. So I was falling behind in mortgage payments. I considered all my options:

1. Selling some of my houses with adequate equity to yield enough capital
2. Obtaining some capital to maintain the payments by getting second trust deeds on one or more of the better houses.
3. Returning some of the problem properties to the lenders

None of the three options was very pleasant. For example, if I opted for the first, I would be selling in a down market and would get lowball offers. Also, only my best houses had adequate equity to yield any capital after selling expenses. I did not want to sacrifice my best houses.

With option two, I feared, I would have to commit to a very high interest rate on a second trust deed. This option could very quickly result in a worsening of the problem.

So I went with option three and contacted some of my lenders so I could cooperate in any way possible. The lenders' response was uniform: all told me to shut up and keep paying on their mortgage. Lenders typically will respond to owner-occupied property issues but assume we investors have deep pockets and will eventually pay. I responded that this was not possible; I just didn't have the funds, and I would offer a deed in lieu of foreclosure in order to cooperate and shorten their foreclosure process.

Some lenders saw a benefit. Other lenders saw the foreclosure process as a "cleansing process" of the title, as any minor liens would be removed in a foreclosure.

Deed in lieu of foreclosure is sometimes called the first cousin to a foreclosure, but it does show that you are attempting to cooperate with lenders, and the credit ding is not quite as serious. Anyway, I lost several houses to some type of foreclosure, and I was forced to be on the sidelines—not in the game to further expand my real estate portfolio.

It took a couple of years and perfect credit—starting with making all mortgage payments on time—before lenders would consider my mortgage application again.

COVID Worldwide Affects

It was about a month or so after I had sent out annual rent increase notices that the government issued its COVID business shut-down notice. I looked at all the factors and was concerned, especially because my rents were considerably lower than surrounding equivalent houses. I needed these rent increases. However, I issued a notice to rescind the rent increases to all of my tenants.

In this notice I explained how dangerous and threatening COVID was to all of us and how we needed to pull together as citizens of the world, so I would rescind the rent increase to do my part. Further, I used this as an opportunity to encourage my tenants to get vaccinated, stating that if they weren't vaccinated, our handymen probably would not enter their homes and do any required work. We did need to protect our handymen from any unnecessary risk. The many tenants I conversed with very pleased with the notice of recission, of course, and were planning vaccinations.

Real Estate Crash of 2008

After the severity of the 2008 downturn was obvious, I did contact several of my lenders and ask for a loan modification. Unfortunately, so did a few million other American mortgage holders, and most of them were owner-occupied. I was very frustrated in that I never had any response from any of the lenders on my request for loan modification. I did complete many forms, both online and written.

I had one agent friend within a bank with whom I had discussed other issues, so I tried repeatedly to reach him. Finally, after many attempts, he took my call. He said "Yes, Daryl, you're a trusted customer, so I will have an off-the-record conversation with you. We are absolutely swamped with applications for loan modification, so I doubt we, or any other mortgage institution, will do a loan modification for you as an investor. We're processing the modifications as fast as we possibly can for owner-occupied so we don't put homeowners out on the street. I seriously doubt any lender will have the time or the interest in processing a loan modification from you as investor."

I thanked him for his sincerity and promised I would never acknowledge the conversation to his management. So I had to consider my current predicament regarding my houses. Unlike previous recessions in real estate in the IE, I was not especially overextended, but no one had expected or predicted the exaggerated level of the real estate crash in the IE. Anyway, my wife, Jacqueline, came home from teaching one day and said, "I heard an advertisement on the radio that we should consider."

So I looked up bankruptcy attorneys specializing in real estate. I called several, and one of them made me an offer I could afford. So we initiated a Chapter 11 bankruptcy reorganization after examining all of my properties. There would be eleven properties—well less than half of my properties—included in the Chapter 11, as they were well upside-down in loan-to-value. For example, one house in Rialto had the highest loan, $280,000, and the property after the 2008 crash was worth $140,000. Other examples were even more severe.

Anyway, the same lenders who wouldn't listen to my pleas for a loan modification now were quite willing to negotiate—actually had to negotiate. My attorney was one of the best and did an excellent job on what we referred to as the "cram down." In this procedure, the loan amount is crammed down from existing value to current value. Total cram down was an almost $1 million decrease in my real estate mortgage debt.

My mortgage debt was now manageable, and PITIMM indicated positive cash flow. From there, new loans were established. Actually, this was rather without the usual paperwork, just the Chapter 11 documentation, which gave me new loans at a reasonable interest rate compared to prime for a non-owner-occupied investor: 5.25 percent.

Of course, Chapter 11 bankruptcy reorganization is a last resort.

Since Delinco is a dba (doing business as), it is eligible for Chapter 11 business rather than Chapter 7, personal bankruptcy. However, the housing crash of 2008, caused by reckless banking practices, put many of us investors in dire straights financially. Certainly it did put me out of the game and on the sidelines for a few years as far as acquiring more property, as few lenders will consider your application while you're in bankruptcy reorganization.

Through this process, I was able to keep almost all of my houses. I lost a couple of houses that were alligators anyway, as they were already most of the way to foreclosure when I filed. After the Chapter 11, I waited too long—four years—to file the discharge. It appears lenders will again consider you two years after you file discharge, assuming you've maintained excellent credit.

Anyway, no one, or hardly anyone, starts a business with the intent of going bankrupt. Again, this was a Chapter 11 reorganization on well less than half of my houses. I was certainly very reluctant to follow this procedure and did so only after repeated rejections, or more likely being totally ignored, on my applications for loan modification.

The Chapter 11 business bankruptcy is considered a restart, a reorganization, to your business. Certainly, it is a very common practice in American businesses. Some years ago, most of the airlines had gone Chapter 11. I am told the Greeks favored Donald Trump getting elected president, as they stated, "He's been bankrupt more often than we have." I do offer this information reluctantly, as it is a possible cure for the ultimate downturn.

CHAPTER 14

Trends Are Your Friends

Borrowing a catchphrase from the stock market, trends are your friends, and if you can properly follow the current trend, your investment should be more profitable. Yes, I admit I'm somewhat cynical in quoting Mr. Galbraith's famous statement equating economic forecasters with astrologers, given my original complaint that no real estate forecaster warned us of the crash of 2008. That one is especially painful, as with proper advice, I would have sold three or four properties in 2007 then made out like a bandit by buying more in 2008. As stated earlier, I was concerned about the rapid increase in real estate values, and especially concerned when I heard firsthand from my niece and others about the reckless banking practices.

While others contend you can buy real estate with nothing down, I contend you can be much more aggressive and successful, and especially improve your negotiating position, with more capital. My current intent with the stock market is to amass more capital for my next real estate investment (see below). From my very positive cash flow, I have invested more of our money in the stock market. From there, I read and watch all business sources for economic trends.

As noted, trends in the stock market are very short-term, while real estate investors are looking for more big-picture, long-term trends. When my wife asks me what I'm doing with our money now, I pick up my guitar and play the Beatles classic "Day Tripper," modifying the words to "Day Trader." Those who have heard me sing plead never again, comparing me to the offspring of Bob Dylan and Rod Stewart.

Real Estate Crash of 2008

It's 2022 Why should we be concerned about the real estate crash of 2008? All important parameters are different now. I choose to review this disastrous episode because real estate is cyclical, and what we see today will change. Interest rates, house values, loan policies, tax policies, and often legislation change to accommodate or reciprocate.

The goal was noble enough: helping more Americans qualify for home ownership. So lenders dropped many of their standards, accepted stated income without employment verification, and would often loan up to 105 percent of the house's value. Supposedly, this extra 5 percent was to upgrade the house. Marty Prince, a long-term veteran as owner of Mortgage Technology, mentioned the "loan 125" as meaning banks would offer second trust deeds up to 125 percent of the home value.

My niece Sonsie worked as a loan processor for one of the biggest mortgage offenders, Countrywide, and she told me about one house that was refinanced multiple times in one year at 105 percent of value. Further, from my niece, "The ARM loans were designed to have smaller payments up front for the first few years and then a huge 'bubble' payment loan at the end (rates were to be at market since these weren't fixed loans), which caused a lot of people to have huge, unaffordable bubble payments due that they couldn't pay once the market crashed. Hence, so many people lost their homes. There were a lot of unethical things happening in the mortgage industry leading up to 2008." During legal proceedings, this same mortgage company was found with hundreds of unprocessed loan modification applications.

With reckless banking policies like these, unqualified borrowers in houses that were already overencumbered by 105 percent loans yielded an inevitable crash. In the Inland Empire (Riverside and San Bernardino counties), there are a higher percentage of non-owner-occupied houses, so a crash such as this is exaggerated. I remember one house that was listed for $253,000, and then came the crash. A month later, a neighboring similar house was listed for drastic sale at $90,000. Both were in equivalent condition. That is how fast and how far the market fell in the IE.

Prize-winning economist John Kenneth Galbraith tells us "the only function of economic forecasting is to make astrology look respectable." I find that especially applicable to real estate forecasters, as the strongest comment I could find in 2007 regarding the pending real estate market was "we may see a slight downturn in 2008." I was searching all sources, as I had noticed the rapid increase in real estate values over the previous three years and was aware of some of the reckless banking practices supposedly with the noble cause of making home ownership more affordable for all. In San Bernardino County, where there is a high percentage of non-owner-occupied properties, there was a full depression. Property values in many areas lost 60 percent of their 2007 value.

Local Economics and Macroeconomics

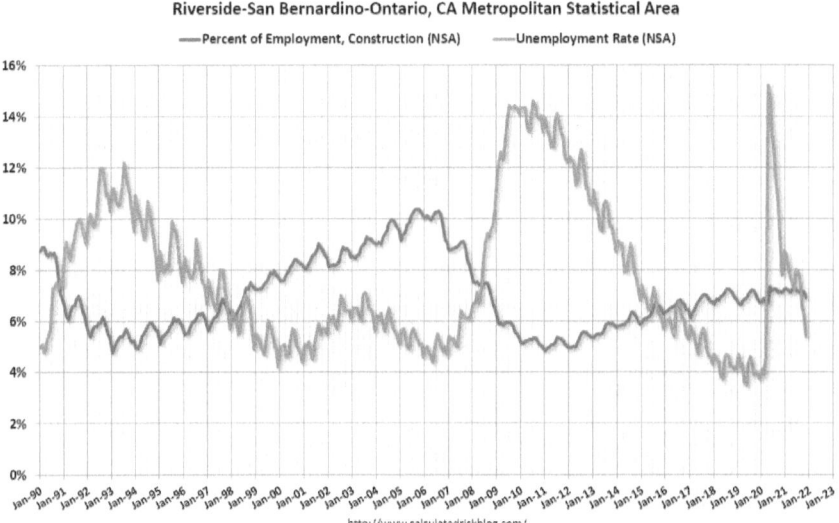

Source: https://www.calculatedriskblog.com/

Generally, I try to invest in an area at a time when the unemployment rate is 9 percent or less. There's no special significance to 9 percent; it's just that my history in investing seems to show that greater than 9 percent could or would be a problem, with tenants being laid off or having decreased hours. Meanwhile, an unemployment rate of 9 percent or less allows me to continue with the program of annual rent increases.

Rent increases, no surprise, usually have an inverse relationship with the unemployment rate. As the unemployment rate decreases, rents in an area will usually increase. Everyone is working and can pay rent, and people want their own domicile. Other factors can be involved, so this is not a hard and fast, totally dependable relationship.

Ken Finds a Local Economic Boom

I hadn't heard from my friendly competitor Ken in a year or so, so I called.

"Got a job promotion with a competitive company but had to move to Chicago," he told me.

"I know you—you have to keep investing. So what's your plan now?" I asked.

He confirmed, "Right call."

Ken explained that he did not find Chicago a desirable area to invest but instead mentioned a midsize town in the Midwest in which there was a recent announcement of a major automobile plant being built. This greatly expanded employment opportunities, hence increasing housing needs and yielding higher rents and property values for most real estate in the area. He was slowly "cashing out" his investments in the Inland Empire, California, and expected to have about $900,000 to invest in this new area.

Ken continued, "Couldn't follow your advice of living within one hour's drive of your investment property, so I went with your plan B and got a second phone number in that area code. From there, I interviewed several and found a trusted real estate agent/property manager. Bought several investment properties. Anyway, I visit quarterly, book my flights a month in advance so they're cheap, and go midweek so I won't miss the family.

"Next, I've seen your notices you've left on your investment properties, so to show a presence, I have followed that strategy whenever I visit. I find some notice to leave on each of my properties. Overall, it is working. Investment property values are already up 20 percent in anticipation of the increased need for housing, and when the manufacturing plant is completed, it should go up another 30 percent."

I contacted Ken again when he was about three years into this project of buying investment property in this midsize city where the major automobile manufacturing plant had been built. As predicted, Ken confirmed that both rents and property values had increased about 25 percent per year. He bought both houses and a small apartment building, and when pressed for details, he did confirm his equity gain had been over $1 million.

Sorry, I can't give more details about the exact geography, as Ken swore me to secrecy to avoid competition as he expands. Actually, Ken said more than just that. Acknowledging this book effort, he said, "Let your new real estate investors do their own research." So I do encourage you to research the area in which you want to invest and maybe work outside your usual area or go a distance when you see a major a reason why an area will need additional housing very quickly. Note what Ken found: a large automobile manufacturing plant being built in a midsize city. There can be many other reasons for an area to have major housing-increase requirements.

Local real estate agents can be quite informative, but obviously, they're playing their angle. I usually have discussions with at least three top agents and ask for documentation or references when appropriate.

Affordability Index

Another interesting parameter in evaluating an area for potential investment is the affordability index. *Affordability index* typically compares the price of housing in an area versus a baseline measure of personal income. Of course, the key parameters here are the median price of homes, the average income, and the current interest rate.

Again, we're looking for trends in the affordability index. An affordability index above 50 percent usually indicates an area that is not inclining but is more likely to be stable or declining in real estate values, as more than 50 percent of the average households can afford to buy a house there. This can be a very misleading parameter, however. For example, in Orange County, many of us have accrued considerable equity in our existing home and can transfer that to the purchase of a new home. Otherwise, just based on our income alone, we could not afford to buy the home we want in Orange County. Then, in adjacent Inland Empire, a higher percentage of the homes are owned by investors, so the affordability index can be higher and prices are still holding or increasing.

The National Association of Realtors considers this parameter very important, as they publish monthly the composite housing affordability index. Note that during times of high inflation, the Fed will step in and increase interest rates, which causes an immediate decline in this composite housing affordability index.

As prices incline in an area, the affordability index will necessarily decline. As investors, we expect to be buying in an area of inclining prices and hence a declining affordability index. We need to study this incline and determine when prices will flatten or reverse. Again, buying a house when prices are flat can be expensive and counterproductive due to the cost of buying and selling property. If the property you bought a year ago has not increased in value, you have lost money due to the cost of buying.

Considering commissions, escrow, and upgrades, sellers' costs are often 10 percent. Buyers pay escrow and loan fees as well as commissions, but their costs are usually closer to 6 percent. As always, these are generalities. If FoSBO, of course, no commissions. As investors, we need an inclining market to at least offset these buyers' costs. If the market is flat, we are buying at a loss due to these costs.

Who Is Building, How Many Units, Where, and Why

As I write this, the title of the lead article in today's economy section of the *Orange County Register* Sunday edition is, "Millennials driving demand for single family rentals." The article goes on to offer information on Sancerra Communities, a new housing developer with five build rent projects planned throughout California, mostly in the IE. The first project in Riverside is for 163 townhomes.

Next, a recent title to a section of our local paper states, "Multiple units being built for rental house rentals." This one goes on to state that a major housing contractor has obtained permits for building five subdivisions in the IE. The first one will be 163 units, specifically townhouses. The size of the units is unclear. Their survey service stated that the impact of the 2008 through 2012 housing crash was still being felt in the IE, and there would be demand for housing.

Specifically, this real estate developing company CEO says they want to offer townhomes for several reasons, including offering additional security to the single parent and offering community amenities you wouldn't get on any private residence. What they don't state is that they can put more units on the same acreage than would be possible with single-family homes. Also, a single-family home always offers more privacy.

Sancerra Communities is not going to invest this amount of money without assurances that there is a demand for rental housing. They refer to Maryland-based real estate consulting company RCLCO, which recently estimated that 2.5 million more single-family rentals will be needed during the next decade to meet growing demand.

Having been through the ups and downs of housing demands in the IE, I am optimistic yet concerned. Perhaps if they put in all five of these units, the IE will be overbuilt and there could be a glut of housing, causing a downturn. Also, I would be more comfortable if the consultant were local rather than east-coast based.

Returning to the basic economic concept of supply and demand, Sancerra's construction plans and RCLCO report certainly indicate that the demand for what we investors are offering—housing—is there and increasing. This positive big-picture outlook is needed for the area in which we plan to invest.

Flipping Houses

In my lengthy career in real estate investing, I've always tried to stay current with the times by attending any conference on a trendy topic. One such seminar sticks in my mind. The advertised speaker was guaranteeing that we would all become millionaires by flipping houses. I listened carefully, and it sounded enticing. Sure, you buy a house worth $400,000, but you buy it for $250,000, flip it, and even with buying and selling cost, you walk away with at least $80,000 profit.

Sound too good to be true? After attending this conference, I certainly agreed that I needed to get to the truth. As with all free seminars, there's a reason they are free. The speaker and his agency want you to sign up for his course and pay big bucks to learn his procedure.

I was not popular at this seminar, as my questions were inappropriate, like, "So how do you find these properties at 40 percent under value?" The speaker insisted I take his course to learn the secrets to finding properties that people will sell to you at 40 percent under value. I persisted, adding to my unpopularity with the speaker.

He finally revealed that you need to find somebody who has no idea of the current property value, or somebody trapped in a divorce situation, or someone simply desperate to get rid of a piece of property. And you have to be in the right place at the right time.

I persisted, adding to my unpopularity with the speaker but with support from other attendees. "In flipping houses, you need to pay both seller's and buyer's costs, which can be 10 percent and 6 percent respectively, as well as the short-term capital gains tax at the maximum rate, right?"

I'm sure at this point, he wanted to tell me to shut up, as this was a free seminar. Instead, he politely again told me to sign up for the course and learn more. As expected, there was no comment on having to pay the maximum tax rate of short-term capital gains, but your CPA will confirm.

As you may have surmised, I'm not a proponent of flipping houses. Compared to my real estate plans, it is extremely high risk, with a great deal of money needed upfront. I don't doubt that it can work in certain circumstances, but apparently you must find someone desperate to unload a property and extremely naïve about its true value. I mean *extremely* naïve, as today it takes about thirty seconds to Zillow search the property. And finally, be ready to exploit this possibly unfortunate person quickly.

Note that in most states, for real estate agents to make an offer at significantly under fair market value, they must state exactly that. Agents who make an offer on a property significantly under fair market value and don't emphatically state that in the offer can be sued or lose their license or both.

So anyway, if you are fortunate enough to identify and buy a house significantly under market value for any reason, I have to believe it would be more profitable to upgrade it and turn it into a rental house, at best rent. Then keep it over a year to avoid short-term capital gains and sell when needed for the lesser long-term capital gain. Uncle Sam disapproves of short-term investments, and he expresses his discontentment through a severe tool: short-term capital gains tax, a maximum-rate tax applied to any investment—real estate or stock market—held for less than one year.

Finally, they won't always tell you this, but flipping houses is most successful during times of, and in an area of, strongly inclining values. How do you know when this strongly inclining market may level off, or worse, reverse? Remember, the definition of a real estate speculator is one fool selling to a bigger fool. You don't want to be that bigger fool.

Buying Foreclosures

Depending on the real estate climate, seminars on buying foreclosures will sometimes appear. There are many ways to buy foreclosures. I think the best way is direct from the bank, as a bank will offer a bargain price and often a short-term loan.

We tried directly contacting borrowers after a public notice of foreclosure was filed, but too often they distrusted us or thought their fairy godfather would suddenly appear to financially bail them out. Seriously, they just were not ready to do business with a stranger and consider a better option.

Seminars on foreclosures were more informative than those on flipping, and offered various ways to buy foreclosures. However, they rarely fully informed you that usually full cash was needed, so this is an activity for the experienced and well-funded. I'm told that Arizona and other states sometimes have auctions at the courthouse, and big profits are obtained by those with the required cash.

To my knowledge, all foreclosures are sold on an as-is basis, so any level of upgrades can be required. Inspect thoroughly, and maybe employ a building engineer, when possible.

When needed, in certain economic times, the banks will maintain what they call an REO list—real estate owned. From there, investors contact the area manager to request a copy of this list of bank-reclaimed properties and can buy directly from this list. Again, often, the bank will offer a short-term loan. Usually, the REO list is already bargain-priced, so no negotiation is acceptable.

Bank policies seem to change with the economic times. Last I remember contacting one of my REO managers who always had a list of houses for me, he countered by saying, "We are now not maintaining a list." Instead, he offered a real estate broker who was listing all of their reclaimed properties. I wasn't interested, as with exposure to the full market, no particular bargain would be available.

Adding an ADU

The governor of California signed legislation to increase affordable housing in California. Part of this bill allows more accessory dwelling units (ADUs) to be added to the same lot. These go by many different names throughout the US, including accessory apartments, secondary suites, Jesus rooms, and granny flats. ADUs can be converted portions of existing homes, such as a garage; additions to new or existing homes; new stand-alone accessory structures; or converted portions of existing stand-alone structures. Throughout the US, other areas have local plan recommendations and zoning standards for ADUs, as the concept of expanding affordable housing is much more than just California's plan.

Similar to the concept of the tough shed I added many years ago to other smaller houses (see chapter 7), this allows us to add ADUs to our existing units at perhaps minimal cost with guaranteed permitting. Is it possible to add an ADU to a house or other existing unit, then rent to two separate parties? Rent or sell as a duplex? I'm not sure if these new laws have fully answered these questions, but they are certainly a possible way for landlords to expand without buying more property, by renting to more people or parties.

Affordable Housing

Following the California legislation intended to increase affordable housing, many communities in Southern California now have a requirement for affordable housing, as so many families, especially young couples, have been priced out of home ownership near where they work. Not sure how that could benefit us as real estate investors; perhaps if we can do some real estate development. So my current plan is offering a triplex on a standard single-family lot.

Going to some contractors, I can get a two-story triplex with a three-car garage built for about $750,000. Each unit would be two small bedrooms, a bath and a half. Should be easy to get permitted due to this demand for affordable housing. Not sure where I would set the rents initially to meet these affordable housing guidelines, which vary from community to community.

Anyway, I can certainly increase the rents in the near future. I think a unit like a triplex would be immediately profitable for resale, but as is my habit, I would keep it for some years. I need the depreciation, and I'm confident rents will continue increasing.

Working Remotely

Also trending today is the acceptance of working remotely. When businesses were closed due to COVID, in order to stay in operation, they allowed many employees to work remotely. Instead of person-to-person meetings, we had Zoom meetings. Other results were shown by webinars and other remote presentations.

How does this trend affect us in real estate investing? Real estate values in the Inland Empire, for example, have increased by 30 percent—much more than in the surrounding counties. Someone reporting to a company in Los Angeles or Orange County can now live in the Inland Empire and work remotely. As a possible example, a party who can afford only a two-bedroom one-bath condo in expensive Orange County can buy a three-bedroom, two-bath home in Fontana and maintain the same employment.

This makes the "Dean plan" of real estate investing more viable. You can change residences and move into the area you want to invest in while reporting to the same employer, as you are working remotely. Today, many of us don't need to live near our place of employment.

A Casino in My Neighborhood

Certainly there are mixed interpretations of the real estate results of a casino in the neighborhood, I think more negative than positive. There is one school of thought that the casino will bring in more traffic certainly, and more jobs. So if you have units to rent, chances are there will be a local bump in employment and more prospective tenants.

Overall, however, most would expect a decline in real estate values near the casino. So maybe a stronger rental market but reduced appreciation of real estate values? A representative of the National

Association of Realtors adds this negative comment: "Casinos are an attractive nuisance, nuisances on home values."

In conclusion, this certainly deserves further attention and scrutiny before we invest in an area near a planned casino. A lower-income area can only benefit, but for other areas, it is perhaps the opposite or neutral.

Governor Banning Evictions

Finally, there is a new trend that is anything but a real estate investor's friend: governors banning evictions. In response to COVID outbreaks, the governors of California and other states have banned evictions temporarily. Supposedly, there is funding to pay the rent, but most landlords complain they have not seen any of this funding, and they have lost rent money due to the eviction ban.

Hopefully, this will be temporary. In my thirty-plus years of real estate investing, this was the first occurrence of banning evictions, and due to a severe worldwide pandemic. We hope the future holds less government interference, especially in such a one-sided manner, allowing tenants to live for free at the owner's expense.

As we move past the COVID pandemic, we need to use any political influence to avoid further government interference in our real estate business. My lawyer colleagues who also invest in CA real estate, assure me that our rental contracts should be binding, fair compensation due both parties.

WhatsApp

Unlike in the stock market, most important parameters change slowly in real estate. However, in today's world, we want immediate access to all important news. Hence, I have started a WhatsApp for real estate investors in Southern California. It's a forum for current trends in real estate, including the following:

- new and alarming laws that the socialists are attempting to use to control our properties
- tax laws that could benefit or hinder
- new construction projects that could benefit or hinder
- financial updates both on interest rates and lending policies
- other pertinent economic or real estate news

Invited to join, hopefully to offer latest info or links, are other real estate investors, property managers, CPAs, mortgage brokers, real estate agents, and anyone else who may offer pertinent information. While much of the information provided is of general usage throughout the US, we will attempt to be specific to Southern California in certain aspects.

www.ingramcontent.com/pod-product-compliance
Lightning Source LLC
Chambersburg PA
CBHW021445210526
45463CB00002B/641